Second Edition

Positively Outrageous Service

OTHER BOOKS BY T. SCOTT GROSS

Why Service Stinks . . . and Exactly What to Do About It!

MicroBranding: Build a Powerful, Personal Brand & Beat Your Competition

*Borrowed Dreams: The Roughest, Toughest Jobs on the Planet . . . And What
I Learned from Working Them*

OUTRAGEOUS! Unforgettable Service . . . Guilt-free Selling

How to Get What You Want from Almost Anybody

Second Edition

Positively Outrageous Service

HOW TO DELIGHT AND ASTOUND YOUR CUSTOMERS AND WIN THEM FOR LIFE

T. Scott Gross

Dearborn™
Trade Publishing
A **Kaplan Professional** Company

Vice President and Publisher: Cynthia A. Zigmund
Acquisitions Editor: Jonathan Malysiak
Senior Managing Editor: Jack Kiburz
Interior Design: Lucy Jenkins
Cover Design: Scott Rattray, Rattray Design
Typesetting: Elizabeth Pitts

Published by Dearborn Trade Publishing
A Kaplan Professional Company

Printed in the United States of America

04 05 06 10 9 8 7 6 5 4 3 2

Library of Congress Cataloging-in-Publication Data

Gross, T. Scott.
    Positively outrageous service : how to delight and astound your customers and win them for life / T. Scott Gross.—2nd ed.
        p.   cm.
    Includes index.
    ISBN 0-7931-8823-7 (pbk.)
1. Customer services. I. Title.
    HF5415.5.G76 2004
    658.8′12—dc22

2004012316

THIS IS DEDICATED . . .

. . . to the one I love. All right, call in the Mamas and the Papas, cue the musicians, and lower the lights to a blue stage wash. That should set the mood for me to tell you about the best partner a man could have, a woman who I have dragged kicking and screaming from one adventure to another. She has never wavered. She has been the brains in addition to the beauty, and she has worked so hard I have often felt guilty. Her name is Melanie but you can call her Buns. This book and all that I do are dedicated to her, the one I love.

If you are waiting for a big-name author or consultant to formally introduce this book, just skip to the first chapter and dive right in. We could have asked one of our big-time, high-profile acquaintances we barely know to write the Foreword, but why? Instead, we asked someone with real credibility to do the honors. We asked a friend who knows us personally and can attest to how POS actually mirrors who we are and how we do business. We asked someone who has witnessed firsthand the power of Positively Outrageous Service. So here's a little testimonial to whet your appetite.

It had been a long week on the road, and as usual I was running through the San Francisco airport trying to catch a flight that would take me home. While hurrying to my plane, I happened to notice a copy of *Positively Outrageous Service* at a bookshop on the concourse and was arrested by the title. I thought, *Positively Outrageous Service. That's exactly what I do for my customers!*

I picked up a copy and started to read at the gate. In fact, I was so involved that had the gate agent not said, "Mr. Vang, have you decided not to go home?" I would have most likely missed my flight.

I had nearly finished the book by the time we landed in Albuquerque and saved what remained until I had completed the long drive home to Santa Fe. By the end of the weekend, I had a dozen new ideas and had made the decision to share *Positively Outrageous Service* with my friends and clients. POS turned out to be more than a good idea; it could determine the success or failure of most businesses. I have since given dozens of copies of *Positively Outrageous Service* and Scott's subsequent books to friends and associates in the hope that they too will discover POS.

Since that first reading, Scott (and Melanie) and I (and Martha, my wife) have met on many occasions, both at his home and in Santa Fe. We have spent many hours sitting on the portal (porch in other parts of the country) sharing stories and ideas. Scott always seems to be preparing for the next book, the next twist on Positively Outrageous Service. He sucks up every story, asking what happened next, what did you do, how did they respond, how did it all turn out. As you will see in a matter of pages, Scott loves great stories.

If you are already a master of serving the customer, you will love this book, as I do. It will give a name and substance to what you may have been doing instinctively. If your business could use a little boost, then this book is also just what you need. There isn't a business anywhere that wouldn't benefit from a good shot of Positively Outrageous Service! If you can warm the customer's heart, the rest is easy!

A.M. Vang, Automotive Consultant
Santa Fe, New Mexico

Contents

THE BIG "DO OVER"

We were ten and five. I was the oldest, and my brother Steve was number two in what would eventually become a small tribe of happy boys. Steve, we called him Beaver after the TV show *Leave It to Beaver,* was my best buddy, even though I didn't know it at the time. We were always wrestling and chasing—typical boy stuff.

Whenever Mom or Dad would fire up the oil-burning beater of a Studebaker, Beaver and I would race to claim shotgun. If you are young, or a girl, that's the right front passenger seat, a pretty desirable prize in the days when all air-conditioning was the 255 system—two open windows at 55 mph!

"I call shotgun!" was what it would take to claim the throne, until we invented "reverses," later "recharges," and still later "backs" as we used up all the words we knew that could indicate a change of intent.

Our contest for shotgun would often go like this:

"I call shotgun!"

"Reverses! Now I call shotgun!"

"No! I call recharges! It's mine!"

And later we would call it all in one breathless phrase as we raced to the car, "I call shotgun, no reverses, no recharges, no backs!"

Life in the 1950s and 1960s was a magical time when reverses and recharges could change the course of an afternoon. They were our own little version of "do overs," that self-offered forgiveness that kept foul balls just inside the first base line and erased a really bad toss when we were flipping for baseball cards in a heated game of "keepers."

So imagine for a moment that you write your first book and surprisingly it's a bit of a hit. You sell a hundred or so thousand copies, and suddenly you get mail from around the world and, once in a while, are even recognized in airports. People call and invite you to exotic conference sites and make you the center of attention. And, just when you are about to ask how much this lavish treatment will cost, they hand a check to you!

Wow! Talk about a rush! When a kid born in Kentucky (the only state where socks and underwear are totally optional . . . don't worry, I have my socks!) gets this kind of treatment, the only possible, logical thought is, "Good golly, I hope they don't find me out!"

For over a decade of speaking on Positively Outrageous Service, I have been hoping my clients would not meet me in person before I took to the stage. In person one-on-one, I am certain they will find me a miserable disappointment. But if I could just get to the stage and let the stories tell themselves, they will see a thing of beauty. They will see Positively Outrageous Service.

A speaker friend once said that writing a book is like flushing a toilet (not an elegant analogy but pretty darned accurate). You write a book that pretty much includes everything you know and that fills about 300 typewritten pages for the average human! And then you are empty. There is nothing else to say until the tank refills. And that is when you discover that there really was more to say, and maybe some of what you said before could use a little tweaking.

It's not like there is something wrong with the original *Positively Outrageous Service;* it's just that I've learned a lot in the past decade. I've learned as much from my audiences as they have learned from me. My experience as a businessperson who meets a payroll has matured. And others, thinkers great and not-so-great, have contributed to the science and art of terrific customer service. So I have wanted to take back all the copies of the original *Positively Outrageous Service* and make a few adjustments.

Then . . . one magical day my editor called and offered me a "do over." This is my "do over," and you may as well be told up front that there are plenty of things I did so right the first time. I married the best woman on the planet. I call her Buns, and she still loves me! I have a son who is good inside and out. We call him Kiddo. I have a wonderful, handpicked daughterette that I affectionately call Jo Bob. And last, there are two wonderful grandchildren, Big Guy and Little Princess. For none of them would I call a "do over."

You're going to meet them as you read, and if you are wondering why a business writer would include stories about his family in a serious business book, there are a couple of things you need to know.

Positively Outrageous Service isn't something you do, it's something you are! And while POS (the insider's term for Positively Outrageous Service) is serious business, this isn't a serious business book. That's right. If you don't want to have fun, this book and POS aren't for you!

Now get yourself ready to discover the serious fun of loving on customers—even the ones who wait for you at home.

"I call shotgun! No reverses, no recharges, no backs!"

POS

An Affair of the Heart

1

IN THE BEGINNING

"Any fool can give away product but it takes brains to sell it."

I apologize for not remembering the author of the quote, but when I first read that beautiful line we were neck-deep in a fast-food restaurant franchise that was going down the tubes in a hurry. Our product was good, our prices were competitive, and our service? It was spot on! Too bad I couldn't say the same for our sales. And then we discovered POS!

This book simply must begin with a story, maybe two.

ROBERTA

One bitingly cold Denver morning I was to speak at the convention center, when we discovered that there were no batteries for my wireless microphone. No problem. There was time enough for me to find one at a local store. Well, there was one problem. It was 5 degrees outside, minus 25 when you figured in the wind chill factor, and absolute 0 if you factored in a Texan's thin blood.

The morning radio DJ had warned that the bitter cold was dangerous, especially if you were elderly or had respiratory problems. I would have been forgiven for staying put, but I'm not elderly and don't have respiratory problems, and I had an audience that needed to be served.

I had volunteered and that was that. Without thought, I found myself setting off into blowing snow along streets made dangerous by a thin coating of ice and a howling wind all in the cause of a battery.

Around the corner, I found a 7-Eleven, my battery, and this wonderful story. Inside the store I noticed there were two people, one behind the counter. Her name was Roberta. At least that was what her nametag announced. She had dark skin, almond eyes, dark neatly styled hair, and a crisply starched 7-Eleven uniform.

Roberta's total attention belonged to the other person in the store, a tall, elderly gentleman who at one time must have been six feet two or perhaps three, but now, in his mid-80s, he walked all hunched over as if bent by the years and a hard life getting harder.

He had a lame leg that he would cast forward, lock into place, and then drag the other up to meet it. I could only imagine how difficult it must be for him to navigate on this bitter cold and icy morning. My noticing came in the form of what felt like a premonition. My gut instinct led me to believe that this guy must come to 7-Eleven every day, buy the same thing every day, and all because, my guess, Roberta was the only person anywhere to treat him like a special human being.

I decided I wanted to be a part of this transaction, if only as an observer with a feeling to verify. I stepped close but not too close.

I watched as the old man placed a banana and a muffin on the counter. He spoke not a word, not then, not the entire time I watched. Instead, he chose to stand as straight as possible.

Roberta rang up and announced a price that I knew her elderly friend already knew. He, in turn, silently slipped a gnarled fingered, age-spotted hand into the pocket of his greatcoat and withdrew a coin purse that was nearly as old as the hand that held it. He tried to hold steady but could not.

Roberta fished out a few small coins and replaced them with a few smaller coins in change. The hand dropped the coin purse back into its pocket, and the other gnarled hand extended and waited for what must to them have been the next step in a familiar dance.

Roberta put the banana and the muffin into a plastic bag, spread the handle as wide as she could, and then gently slipped the handle onto the old man's wrist. Then with her own young, soft hands she warmed his hands as tenderly as I've ever witnessed. Calling him by name, she pulled his scarf a bit closer, buttoned one more button those arthritic hands would have had difficulty with, smiled, and said simply, "Be careful. You know I want to see you again tomorrow."

And without a word, a much warmer gentleman shuffled into a cold, dangerous morning.

"Not what I expect at a 7-Eleven," I said. "Why the special treatment, is he related?"

"He's my customer," she said in a short phrase that explained it all. Then she tossed her hair and smiled. "Oh, thank heaven for 7-Eleven!"

And today, she was right.

Roberta's tale is true and one of my most requested stories. The next story, "The Christmas Man," touches me so deeply that I never tell it from the platform. If you are sensitive, skip to the next section. Otherwise, hang in there! It won't be long before I have you busting a gut laughing!

THE CHRISTMAS MAN

First the scene, Christmas eve at a busy Southwest Airlines gate. The gate agent is suffering from a cold. She is away from her family for the holiday season and feeling as miserable as the weather.

This is a story about angels. Two of them. One is an "angel unaware" named Rachel. The other is named McDonald.

Now, in the words of Angel Rachel: "I looked up and saw the sweetest-looking old man standing with a cane. He walked very slowly over to the counter and in the faintest voice told me that he had to go to New Orleans. I tried to explain to him that there were no more flights that night and that he would have to go in the morning. He looked so confused and very worried.

"I asked if he had a reservation or if he remembered when he was supposed to travel, but he seemed to get more confused with each question. He just kept saying, 'She said I have to go to New Orleans.'

"It took a while but finally I was able to discover that this old man had been dropped off at the curb by his sister-in-law on Christmas eve and told to go to New Orleans where he had family. She had given him some cash and told him to just go inside and buy a ticket.

"When I asked if he could come back tomorrow, he said that she was gone and that he had no place to stay. He then said bravely that he would wait right here until tomorrow.

"Naturally, I felt a little ashamed. Here I was feeling sorry for myself about being alone for Christmas, when this angel named Mr. McDonald was sent to me as a reminder of what being alone really meant. It broke my heart to see him standing there.

"I told him not to worry, that we would get everything straightened out. Cynthia, another agent on duty, helped book him a seat on the earliest flight the next morning. We gave him a senior citizen's fare, which left him a little extra money for traveling. About this time, he started looking very tired, and I stepped around the counter to ask quietly if he was all right. That's when I noticed that his leg was wrapped in a bandage. He had been standing on it the whole time, holding a plastic bag full of clothes.

"I called for a wheelchair, and when it came, we both stepped around to help him in. It was then I noticed a small amount of blood on his bandage. I asked how he had hurt his leg, and he explained that he had just had bypass surgery and that an artery had been taken from his leg. Can you imagine? This man had heart surgery, and shortly afterward had been dropped off at the curb to buy a ticket with no reservation to fly to New Orleans alone!

"I had never really had a situation like this, and I wasn't sure what I could do. I went back to ask my supervisors, Kathy and Mercedes. When they had heard the whole story, I asked if we could find a place for him to stay. They both said absolutely.

"When I came back out, we got his plastic bag of clothes and cane together and gave the nice World Services employee a tip to take him downstairs to wait for the shuttle. I bent down to explain to Mr. McDonald that we had a hotel room for him for the night and a meal ticket for dinner and breakfast. I patted him on the arm and promised everything would be just fine.

"As he was about to be wheeled away, he said, 'Thank you,' bent his head, and started to cry. I cried, too.

"When I went back to thank Kathy, she just smiled and said, 'I love stories like that. He is your Christmas man.'"

THE REAL POSITIVELY OUTRAGEOUS SERVICE

Positively Outrageous Service is a story. It is about the top line and the bottom line. It is the story of how great servers love their customers unconditionally and put big money on the bottom line. It's about how they profit in other ways, too. When an organization adopts Positively Outrageous Service "heart," line, and sinker, there are other changes that are often difficult to describe but impossible to miss.

Positively Outrageous Service is as much about who you are as it is what you do. The nice thing is that when you change what you do, it changes who you are.

THE "UNDER PEOPLE" CONTRIBUTE

A former boss lovingly calls them the "under people" and, to fill out the definition just a bit, let me describe them as just ordinary folks. They are the folks who remain unseen, never too loud, never in the spotlight, just regular folks who bake our bread, press our shirts, change our oil, and otherwise keep the economy moving and the world slowly turning. So I am always happy to shine a light on the folks we rarely see but to whom we owe so much.

These next few stories come from the Hampton Inn. They prove quite nicely that you don't have to wear a suit to be important and don't need a fancy title to make a huge difference in someone's life. Some of our best examples of Positively Outrageous Service come from "under people."

TOOTH FAIRY

A family was vacationing at the Hilton Sedona Resort. As luck would have it, the guests' daughter lost her first tooth while there. Without letting her parents know, the little girl decided to put the tooth under her pillow and left a note saying, "If there is such a thing as a tooth fairy, please let me know." Then the family left to view the Grand Canyon.

During the day, Mabel, a housekeeping attendant, came into the room to clean. When she lifted the pillow, she quickly saw the tooth and read the note left by the little girl. Mabel reflected on the comment "If there is such a thing as a tooth fairy . . . " and imagined that one day she would deal with such subjects as fairies and other childhood things with her own children.

Mabel is a Service Natural and a talented one at that. Mabel drew a picture of what a tooth fairy might look like, wings and all. Then she dug into her tip money to complete the surprise.

Imagine the little girl's delight when she returned to the resort that evening. She looked under her pillow and found a beautifully drawn picture of the tooth fairy, wings and all—and $2.

KEYS, PLEASE!

A guest was delayed by the airline and checked into the Hampton Inn St. Louis Airport very late. Even worse, his luggage did not make it. When the guest arrived at the hotel, he told Steve, the night auditor, of his dilemma. He had a 9 AM meeting and needed to look fresh and clean.

Steve suggested that he go to Wal-Mart because of their late hours. There he could pick up fresh underwear and dress shirts. Since he had flown in and had no way to get there, Steve (you will never believe this) gave the guest directions to Wal-Mart and the keys to HIS car!

In the coming pages, we'll learn how to get ordinary people to deliver Positively Outrageous Service. It's simple, just not easy!

POS DEFINED

With Positively Outrageous Service there really are no rules. If you manage to surprise and delight a customer, how you do it doesn't much matter. But somewhere in my geeky past, I learned that good science is repeatable science. If you cannot make an experiment come out the same way twice, you're playing with a phenomenon not a theory. There are many people—we call them Service Naturals—who instinctively give POS when presented with the opportunity.

For POS to be good science, you have to be able to do it more or less on purpose, not just by shooting from the hip. You need a definition so that you can understand why the cool things you do for customers make such an impression on them. Many Service Naturals, folks who deliver Positively Outrageous Service naturally, have thanked me for giving a name for that service magic they do. And bosses who love POS have said that having a definition for POS has made sharing it with their teams easier and made their POS promotions both more effective and profitable.

Positively Outrageous Service is:

- Random and unexpected
- Out of proportion to the circumstance
- Playful and personal to the customer
- Compelling, leading to positive word of mouth

POS is the service story you can't wait to tell. It is a "wow" delivered on a random basis. If you are expecting it, it is not POS; it's something nice but something else.

"Unexpected" is key to the definition of truly Positively Outrageous Service. The element of surprise and novelty jolts the attention of the customer or patron and creates an experience that's memorable because it is so different from the expectation.

But to "pick" a small "nit," even if you are expecting the unexpected and don't know exactly *what* to expect, I guess you could still call that the unexpected!

Random and Unexpected

You can't give excellent service 100 percent of the time. Mistakes happen. That's a fact of life you cannot ignore. If you can't always give excellent service, how can you expect to always give Positively Outrageous Service? The better question may be, "Why would you want to?"

It may be that attempting to serve every guest, customer, or patron with POS will create an expectation that's nearly impossible to fulfill. Besides, there is something to be said for keeping them guessing.

Of course, you want the customer to be able to depend on you for courteous, fast, accurate, and complete service. But just once, or once in awhile, serve them outrageously, and they will be back expecting your standard good service but hoping perhaps for another chance to be served outrageously.

Once customers have been served outrageously, they will project that experience into every future opportunity you have to serve them. In other words, one bout of POS will color every future interaction. You may be only providing your usual great service, but to the customers, this experience will be colored by their fond memory of the previous Positively Outrageous Service.

Going above and beyond has merit, of course. But why create an expectation you can't possibly meet on a regular basis? In fact, there is a danger in attempting consistent POS. Slip to mere "excellence," and the customer may feel cheated.

The Credit Union Executives Society invited me to speak on a week-long cruise throughout the Caribbean. In the Crow's Nest Lounge towering over the sea at the bow of the ship, my wife, Buns, and I enjoyed consistently excellent service. Our Filipino steward made us feel more than welcome each night as we would watch the sunset over a glass of wine.

His name was Bito. On our second visit, Bito greeted us by name and, by the end of the cruise, was nearly family. We knew about his kids and career living aboard the beautiful New Holland luxury liner. So far, you'd have to call Bito's service excellent.

On our last evening visit, Bito presented us with a hand-printed Dutch maiden's bonnet as a memento of our time together. It was beautiful.

What kind of tip do you think we left?

How would this story be different if I told you that *every* passenger received the same treatment? What if you patronized the lounge and did not receive one?

Phil Romano, a world-class restaurateur, opened an out-of-the-way Italian restaurant called Macaroni's. It's almost as if Phil was actually looking for a place to hide his operation, an independent, not inexpensive restaurant located in the boonies at least 15 miles from downtown and destined for failure.

It didn't fail. The place was packed. Especially on Monday and Tuesday nights, the same nights that most restaurants struggle to keep their doors open.

Here's why. Other than the obvious reason that Macaroni's serves good food, Phil Romano had a gimmick that's based on the old Psych I principle that random reward begets regular behavior. In this case, the behavior is eating at Macaroni's on a Monday or Tuesday night!

The original Macaroni Grill probably seated close to 200, maybe more. But if you dined there on a Monday or Tuesday night and happened to get lucky, you and *every* customer in the joint would receive a letter, instead of the bill.

The letter stated that because the Macaroni's concept was to make people feel like guests, it followed that it seemed awkward to charge guests for their good time. So once each month, on a Monday or Tuesday and always unannounced, everyone ate free! The letter continued with ". . . tonight is your lucky night" and went on to remind customers that the waitstaff was also working for free, so ". . . please treat them generously." Almost as an aside, the diners were asked to tell their friends about Macaroni's.

Would you call that POS? I do!

This practice continued until the business simply outgrew the building. It was booming seven nights a week. Now you can enjoy Macaroni Grill restaurants across the country. But for those of us who watched it grow and watched it go, the original will always be the best.

Eating free is definitely unexpected and by pulling this stunt at random, Romano not only managed to WOW the customer, he also was able to pack the house on nights when other restaurateurs were climbing the walls.

Let's take a marketing break and talk about Romano's strategy. First, his location was definitely out of the way. And worse, it was a single operation outside a major metropolitan area. Electronic media being prohibitively expensive, Romano instead elected to blow his whole advertising budget by comping every ticket in the house once a month.

You could say that by picking up the tab for one out of eight (or nine) Mondays and Tuesdays in a month, he managed a full house on what would normally be a dead night. And one out of eight amounted to a discount of only 12.5 percent. When you also figure that his waitstaff was working off the clock, the discount was even less. If you figure that his true costs, mostly food and beverage, were much less than retail, you get an even clearer picture of Romano's bright idea.

Or look at it this way: One night comped out of 30 and you're down to a 3.3 percent ad budget without considering actual costs. And look who he just put on his payroll—you! Testimonials are said to be one of the most effective forms of advertising. In one fell swoop, Romano got a couple hundred tongues wagging, "You won't believe what happened to us last night!" Effective? You bet!

What would the value of Romano's ploy be if it were always on a Monday instead of a Monday or a Tuesday? Why not just give everybody a 3.3 percent discount all the time? See? *Random* is the operating word.

Random rewards beget regular behavior. In this case, the behavior is going out to dinner at an out-of-the-way restaurant on a stay-at-home night on the off-chance that you may eat free. To his surprised customers, Phil Romano looks like a hero—a rich one.

Out of Proportion to the Circumstance

(This story was sent in by David Currier of Signature Flight Support, Orlando, Florida.)

David McKee, senior VP of human resources for BBA, was checking in with British Airways for a London–New York flight. McKee was running late and on reaching the ticket counter was unhappy to discover that the only remaining seat was a middle seat. He mildly protested and mentioned his ailing leg in the hope of getting a little sympathy and perhaps a better seat.

"Next time, get here earlier," was all he could pry from the agent.

At the gate, McKee took another run at the problem. The gate agent was a pretty, red-haired Irish lass, so McKee put on his best Irish brogue and tried again. He mentioned his bum leg and was surprised to hear her say, "I didn't notice a limp while you were in line. Walk back in line and come up to the counter again."

McKee walked perfectly back to the line, but on turning back the limp suddenly appeared.

"Wait a moment while I call my supervisor," said the girl now sporting an uninterpretable Mona Lisa smile.

When the supervisor arrived, McKee found himself once again under the microscope as he went through the same line-to-gate demonstration. Only this time, the limp had mysteriously transferred itself to the other leg! The supervisor caught on to the playful ruse immediately and declared that the passenger had a severe medical problem that required "minimum time on the aircraft."

McKee was immediately issued a new ticket, a new gate, and a new seat—on the Concorde!

Invites the Customer to Play Or . . .

The third characteristic of Positively Outrageous Service is that it is personal and invites the customer to play or otherwise involves the customer. And the more personal you can get the better.

We had landed in Cincinnati to speak to the Hillman Group, the folks who put nuts, bolts, and fasteners of all sorts in your local Ace or TruValue hardware stores. In the weeks leading up to the engagement, we had several conversations with our client in an effort to get to know them better. (Personalization is a form of POS.) It turns out they were getting to know us as well.

Cincinnati is known for its chili, and, peculiar as it may sound, the locals like it served over steaming spaghetti noodles buried under a mountain of grated cheese. Add a fistful of chopped onions, pour on a healthy dose of hot sauce, and you've got yourself a "four way." Skyline chili is always our first stop, no matter what time of the day. To me, breakfast, lunch, or dinner—anytime is Skyline time.

Apparently the folks at Hillman had noticed.

My antenna for POS must have been out of order or switched to standby by the good folks at the West Chester Marriott. They had recently been named the top Marriott in the United States, and at check-in it was easy to see why.

The desk clerk was a "killer"! When she presented my key, she walked around the counter to hand it to me directly, taking time to ask if I needed recommendations for dinner or directions to local attractions.

During the audio check that afternoon, our client asked if we had plans for Skyline. Yep, we'd already made our first stop, and yep, there remained the possibility of a late-night chili run. I noticed Kim Sherlock from the Marriott seeing my gush for Skyline chili but passed it off to amusement that a guy could get worked up over noodles, chili, and cheese. As it turned out, she was about to become an accomplice in a POS moment.

No more was said, the audio check was completed, and Buns and I went off to dinner. When we returned to our room, we were instantly struck by a large basket wrapped in shiny silver foil and tied enticingly with bright red ribbon.

I opened the card. Buns attacked the ribbon. What was inside? The usual basket of fruit? A cheese and fruit plate? An assortment of local jams and sauces? Nope. It was a treasure! Two cans of Skyline chili, two Skyline mugs, and a gift certificate for even more Skyline!

Perfect!

When you listen to your customers, they will tell you how to make them say wow. And when you wow them in a personal way, it tells them that you are listening and that in turn tells them that they are important to you.

Are cheese and fruit plates unwelcome? No, they just aren't a wow for everybody.

One of our favorite clients called our office asking what it was that turned me on, and prepared a welcome basket of Cheez-It crackers and bottled water. That, to me, was a wow!

The Hampton Inn has it in my profile that I like water and Doritos. Okay, call me a man of pedestrian tastes, but while you are at it, call me a customer of Hampton Inns at every opportunity!

Great POS invites the customer to play or otherwise be personally involved.

And by the way, a basket of Skyline chili, Cheez-Its, or Doritos is bound to cost less than the typical overpriced room service plate of cheese and fruit. And it has considerably more impact!

In Fun

Some businesses have a built-in advantage when it comes to service. Their customers are "in fun" when they arrive. Being "in fun" simply means showing up with the mind-set to be loose and have a good time. People are much more likely to be "in fun" at the ballpark than at the dry cleaners. But smart operators of any business look for opportunities to invite the customer to play.

We own two very different businesses, and you would be surprised at how willing our customers are to join in the fun once we start playing.

As a speaker at conferences and conventions, I find people love to become part of the presentation. You can tease them unmercifully, and they always bounce back asking for more. Audiences love opportunities to get involved physically, give their opinions, and share stories and ideas.

A favorite story happened while speaking at the beautiful Dana Point Resort in Southern California. The audience became highly involved as I hammed it up and described the white chocolate macadamia nut cookies we used to bake fresh at our restaurant. The cookies were distributed at random as a little surprise for our customers. You couldn't buy them; it did no good to ask. We're talking free!

These cookies helped build a second lunch run of high school students. The students never knew exactly when a delicious, hot, wonderful cookie would appear on their tray. So not wanting to miss out, they became regulars.

When our seminar broke for lunch, someone inquired about dessert. "We were hoping Scott would provide some of those delicious cookies" was the response.

Aha! An opportunity to serve up a healthy dose of POS! With a little help from the concierge, we arranged for the owner of Chocolate Soldier, a nearby candy store, to deliver the closest substitute we could find—huge white chocolate macadamia nut clusters.

Notice that not only was I serving outrageously but so was Detra (De) Francis, the owner, who volunteered to make the delivery as soon as she closed the shop.

As my seminar was about to wrap up, in walked De, who was sharply dressed and carrying a beautiful gold foil box with bright red ribbon.

This was unexpected, out of proportion, and highly involving as my obviously pleased and surprised audience got a delicious dose of Positively Outrageous Service.

People love to hear their names and see themselves on video or in photos. I make it a practice to memorize key names and industry-related jargon before I speak, so that I can better target the audience. Dropping a name, teasing a big shot, and telling theater folks about "trailers" and soft drink execs about "figals," are all good techniques for drawing the audience into the action.

When we owned our first restaurant, it was amazing how "playing" with one customer often cued another customer to spontaneously join in the fun. Male or female, businessperson or day laborer, they all enjoyed being invited to play.

Think about it. Doesn't being invited to play make you feel welcome? If being left out of the fun when the older kids went out to play hurt so much as a kid, doesn't it make sense that just being asked to participate can feel so good?

Creates Compelling, Positive Word of Mouth

Positively Outrageous Service is often so unusual that you feel compelled to talk about it.

More than 20 years ago, when this restaurant was still in existence, good friends of ours called excitedly to invite us for dinner at Little Mike's Ice House. Now that name does not conjure up visions of elegant surroundings and impeccable service. In fact, Little Mike's Ice House sounds exactly like the corner convenience store that it was. Who would expect that you could also get authentic northern Italian food and a family-style welcome in a place that sells beer by the quart and, from the outside at least, could hardly deserve a much higher status than "dive"?

In spite of food that turned out to be truly fabulous, my friends could only talk about the service. "Don't be shocked when you see the place," they said. "Wait until you've had a chance to sample the service before you make up your mind."

Sorry, but the neighborhood was so bad I was afraid to leave the car unattended. We stepped around two sidewalk drunks drinking from paper bags to make our way to the oilcloth-covered tables corralled by folding metal chairs.

"Now can I make up my mind?"

"Not yet," they smiled.

Out from behind a wooden screen came a five-foot whirlwind of energy and hospitality saying, "Hi! I'm Anna. Are you hungry?"

"Yes, ma'am."

"Well, you'd better be. I don't like my food to sit on the plate. Do you like meatballs? Of course, you do!" And with a wink, she disappeared only to return with a plate of softball-sized meatballs, steaming hot. You could smell them from ten feet away. I couldn't wait.

"Here you go, honey," she beamed as she stabbed one with a fork and popped it into my mouth. "Once you taste some of Anna's cookin', I've got you hooked."

And she did. So what if it was served on paper plates? So what if you went to the fridge to get your own beer, soda, or wine, from bottles with screw-on caps? At Mike and Anna's, you were made to feel at home, like family. And how many businesses make you feel like that?

"We don't use butter. Use your bread to mop up the sauce. That's what the sauce is for. And you'd better eat it or you'll wear it!"

And, of course, by the end of our first visit, we left as friends and bent low to proudly accept a motherly hug.

(That happened many years ago. Little Mike and his trusted partner Anna are cooking for a different crowd now. I don't know how they could have called it Heaven without them.)

2

MORE POS STORIES

STEP UP TO POS

Mary Burlingame of Executive Beechcraft in St. Louis is a Service Natural. Mary says, "We were in the running for a very important charter flight that was usually someone else's customer, but this customer was willing to give us a chance. This particular woman is very picky, financially able to *be* picky, and carries a staff that continuously says the words, 'How high?' if you know what I mean.

"Her main complaint from years of flying was her inability to walk up the stairs of any aircraft due to failing health. My 'wow' was to take this dilemma to our building maintenance staff, and together we measured the aircraft in question and built a ramp. They not only built it, they also carpeted it and added a handrail!

"It was a very proud accomplishment on our part, but I had to think one step further to make this a legitimate 'WOW'! I called the other FBO, gave them the exact dimensions, and they built a duplicate ramp!

"We continue to keep this customer, although she has graduated to larger aircraft that we must 'farm out' for a 5 percent commission. We have repeatedly suggested that it would be okay for them to charter directly, but they insist on remaining with us to ensure we get our 5 percent . . . just because!

"Ain't life grand when you try just a little harder to be number one?"

RIGHT SHOE, WRONG FOOT

Phyllis Endrich, former VP of the National Shoe Retailers Association, shared this story: A woman approached a Nordstrom sales associate with a complaint about a pair of shoes she had recently purchased and was currently wearing. The salesman needed but a quick glance to determine the cause of the problem. Left shoe, right foot, right shoe, wrong foot!

Rather than embarrass her, he simply asked for her permission to remove the offending shoes so that he might effect a repair. Once in the back room, he began hammering and pounding on the counter. In a few minutes, he returned and gently placed the unaltered shoes on the correct feet!

DOUBLY SWEET

(This is one of my all-time favorite stories of Positively Outrageous Service. I would tell it from the platform, except that I tear up just reading it. I hope you appreciate this story as much as I do. If there is something doubly sad when man is inhuman to man, there is something doubly sweet when a stranger, in this case a planeload of strangers, take just a moment to love one another.)

Jim Hensley of Sleepy Eye, Minnesota, loves his wife. Together, they share the burden of Marcia's kidney disease. That's the bad news. If there is any good news, it might be that, at the time of this story, advances in treatment had freed Marcia from the dreaded kidney dialysis machines, granting her the freedom to travel more than a few miles from her home.

Well, there was still one tether, of sorts: Marcia was on the list for a kidney transplant and that meant never straying too far from a telephone. There is a 20-hour window of opportunity after which the organ is ruled unusable. Use it or lose it, because there are many on the list waiting for suitable organs and far too few usable organs available.

So it was with a lot of excitement and not a little trepidation that Jim and Marcia, armed with a supply of self-dialysis materials, set off on their first real vacation in years.

Didn't you know it would happen?

About the same time the Hensleys were packing their suitcases, a 68-year-old New York man suffered a stroke and died, leaving behind a grieving family plus a kidney that would be a perfect match for Marcia. The kidney was harvested just about the time the Hensleys were boarding their flight. Shortly afterward, a transplant team at the Mayo Clinic began to assemble while at the same time desperately attempting to phone the Hensleys.

No answer, anywhere. A desperate search led to the Sleepy Eye Police Department, which led to the neighbors and a call to Jim's assistant and finally a frantic call to the close friends who would be meeting Jim and Marcia in Palm Springs.

The window was half-closed.

Jim can take it from here: "Somewhere over western Colorado, Northwest Airlines Captain Bruce Beecroft received a call from the Mayo Clinic. A moment later, a NWA flight attendant tapped Marcia on the shoulder and asked, "Are you Marcia Hensley?" When Marcia responded affirmatively, the flight attendant told us that Mayo had found Marcia a kidney and that her surgeon was on the telephone. We were told of the quality of the tissue match and that if we accepted, we had about ten hours to reach the Mayo Clinic. Marcia accepted.

"The first flight to Minneapolis from Palm Springs was at 8 AM the next day, 10 AM central time. Too late. Do we land in Palm Springs, catch a flight to Los Angeles, and take a red-eye back to the Twin Cities? Too risky.

"There was one other option: divert to Las Vegas and catch a flight leaving in two hours that would take us on a trip to health and freedom.

"Captain Beecroft announced, 'We have just received some exciting and wonderful news. One of our passengers has been on a transplant waiting list, and we have just been informed that a kidney has been located. In order to allow the family to return to Minnesota in the allotted time, we will be landing in Las Vegas long enough for them to deplane. We will refuel, take care of some paperwork, and no, you cannot get off and play the airport slot machines.'"

Jim continues, "We exited the plane to applause and comments of encouragement and not a single complaint about the delay from our fellow passengers.

"I sensed something was wrong as we neared the front of the plane, where a grim-faced pilot awaited. As we exited the plane onto the jetway, a member of the NWA ground crew said she had some bad news. A Mayo Clinic representative had called to say the kidney was no longer available. There had been a miscommunication from the donor bank to the Mayo regarding the length of time we had to accept the kidney. Unbeknownst to either Mayo or Marcia, that kidney had been sent to a patient in Seattle.

"What's done is done. In Palm Springs the sun was shining, the temperature was in the mid-70s, the snow-capped mountains surrounded us, and we were with good friends and on vacation."

(Good news! I received a follow-up from Jim Hensley. Marcia did receive a kidney transplant, and in March of 2002 they took their first extended vacation since 1997—to Hawaii. How about that!)

BEN & MARRY

(This came from a Ben & Jerry's newsletter; no author, no date, my words.)

To a crowd of 40 visitors an announcement was made that a pint had been found on the production line that was labeled with the name "Rebecca." When the tour leader retrieved the mysterious container, a breathless Rebecca opened it to find a sparking diamond engagement ring. Naturally, she and her intended were showered with, what else, rainbow-colored sprinkles!

HYATT HOSPITALITY

On a trip to Hawaii, Bill Ponder's Tauck Tours group was booked at the Hyatt Regency. Unfortunately, service at the Hyatt is so good that a number of departing guests didn't! And that left Bill and the remainder of the tour group homeless in Hawaii.

Along came the Hyatt Regency manager, who apologized and presented each disappointed tourist with a lei and a gift. Next came an envelope for each that contained a letter of apology, a cash refund of the $487 they would have spent at the Hyatt, AND confirmed reservations at another hotel with a minimum rate of $385 per night.

Hyatt then proceeded to pay for three nights!

As Bill says, "Talk about Positively Outrageous Service! Can you top this?"

TEN STEPS AHEAD

(This story comes from Tim Wiltshire of Famous Murphys in Reno, Nevada.)

"I needed some new clothes. I was having trouble finding the time in my day to get to the store. I recently had finished reading *OUTRA-GEOUS* (Warner Books, 1998), and you mentioned the Men's Wear-house several times, so I thought I would give them a try.

"I called and spoke to the assistant manager, Abe, at the Reno store. I told him I was short on time and that I would arrive at his store at 3 PM. I asked if he would set out five pairs of slacks ranging from black to brown, 100 percent wool, and high quality. That way, I could drop into the store, choose my favorites, get measured, and be on my way.

"I think that I am five steps ahead of the normal customer." I agree!

"I arrived at the appointed time. Abe met me promptly and took me to the back of the store. He said, 'I'm all ready for you.'

"There on a counter he had lain out not only the five pairs of slacks but also five matching shirts, five matching ties, and five packs of fancy socks to round out the outfits.

"I said, 'WOW!' I thought I was five steps ahead of him, when in fact he was ten steps ahead of me. Needless to say, I bought it all, got measured, and was out of the store in 15 minutes flat!

"I'll be going back there!"

SERVICE AUGMENTATION

(Doc Bradley Garber is a plastic and reconstructive surgeon in Tulsa, Oklahoma, but he could have been the author of this book! Read on, please!)

"Judy, please take this book home and read it over the next couple of weeks. As I have read through this book, there are some important points that we can apply to our practice as well as to our everyday lives as we interact with others outside the work setting.

"Obviously, some things are not applicable to our medical practice, but Dick might enjoy the book as it relates to his business. As you read through this book, I would like you to highlight ten or more points that you consider important. Give the book back to me when you finish, be-cause Chris would like to read it. I want POS and WOW to be ingrained in our practice. We both need to be creative, show our imagination, and engage our customers, so when they leave our office they are 'blown

away' by the positive attitudes and fantastic care and concern we provide. You have been working with me long enough to know how I feel
about our practice. I want you to take the power and exhibit the flexibility that will allow you to take control and provide POS on a daily basis.
Use your common sense, imagination, and positive attitudes to follow
through on our motto, 'Can do, will do, consider it done!'

"Thanks for your great help and loyalty over the years! Take your
family out to eat with this $100—just an example of what POS and
WOW are all about. I want to practice more POS, and you can too!"

Cordially yours,

E. Bradley Garber, MD

(May I add an "Amen"?)

A TRUE LEADER

Bruce Doggett, a Houston-based captain for Southwest Airlines, is a
quiet hero. One late evening while waiting to check in to the crew hotel,
one of Doggett's crew members noticed an elderly woman attempting to
check in short on cash and without a credit card. The woman was visibly
upset at the thought of having nowhere to go. She was obviously exhausted, which only complicated matters. When the waiting crew member realized what was going on, she also noticed that Doggett had left
his position of next in line.

Doing what was for him only natural, Doggett had pulled a second
clerk to the side and was quietly paying for the room.

Said his crewmate, "I was touched at his gesture of extreme kindness
while trying to remain anonymous. I could not just let that go by without
saying something to him, so I waited to let him know how kind it was."

In typical quiet hero fashion Doggett said simply, "What goes around
comes around."

YOU'VE COME TO THE RIGHT PLACE

(Ken Brown of CSM Carlisle Motors, Clearwater, Florida, wrote.)

"I was greeting customers in the morning on our service drive. I
walked up to a van, and as I approached I could just tell that the lady
driving was upset and shaken about something. I said, 'Good morning,'
and asked how I could help. Her voice quivered and she was almost in
tears but she replied, 'This hasn't been a very good day for me.'

"She told me that when she went to get in her van to come to her service appointment, she had a flat tire. After asking a neighbor to help change the tire, she cautiously proceeded to the dealership.

"As she approached an intersection where there had been a multi-vehicle accident, she noticed a car that looked like her husband's. It was. (Bad news) He was fine. (Good news) The vehicle was totaled. (More bad news)

"The distraught women made her way to the dealership expecting a bill for a tire, an oil change, plus the normal wait at the dealership."

Ken says, "I directed her to our waiting area, and then I went to work. I had our mechanic repair her flat tire and put it back on the van, while we changed the oil and filter. I instructed our cashier that Carlisle would take care of her charges for the day, and left a short message on her paperwork saying, 'I hope this will help you have a better day.'

"And I also left a fresh carnation on her dashboard."

THE LADY DOTH PROTEST!

"My name is Deborah S. I ordered a Saturn SC2 from my local dealership on May 10, and it was my understanding that the car would be built on May 30 and delivered in seven to ten days following.

"Well, something was apparently amiss with the sunroof, and my car was not built as scheduled. It was delayed a second time because the factory was not painting cars in the color I ordered. Then it was delayed a third time because other orders were ahead of mine. (Apparently, once you're out of line getting back in is no easy task.) Finally, I guess you guys and gals decided you needed a vacation (1,000 cars a day, whew!), and you closed the factory for two weeks. (I've been holding off my own vacation, hoping I'd have a new car to cruise around in.)

"Now, I understand my car will be built August 2. I'm a part-time college professor. My British lit class has heard all summer of my automobile-related trials and tribulations. At the beginning of the semester, I was as exuberant and excited as one of Shakespeare's love sonnets; now I am melancholy and woeful as Hamlet.

"But hope springs eternal (and so apparently do hackneyed phrases), and my class (ah, youth!) decided to help matters along (photo enclosed showing 'Ms. S. wants her Saturn!' on hand-printed posters). As you can see from the photo and expressed in my words here, we've all kept our sense of humor regarding this snafu. However, I now join my class in their plea, 'Ms. S wants her Saturn!'"

Here's the remarkable reply from corporate: "To build or not to build? That seemed to be the question. While it was 'tis nobler in our minds to never let you suffer the slings and arrows of outrageous delays . . . Or to take arms against a sea of color (fire-engine red, that is!) and by opposing end them. To die, to sleep, to shut down the plant for two weeks. And by shutting down causing you to suffer even more. It was too much and not a consummation devoutly to be wished. Not by us, ever.

"Alas, the fine folks at Saturn of San Antonio joined your class in pleading, 'Please send Ms. S her car!' But some delays even we cannot prevent. And believe us when we say we want your car to be perfect . . . (Saturn included a check for $300 to take Ms. S and her class to dinner.)

"We really are sorry about the delays, but we hope we can turn your 'Hamlet tragedy' into a 'Saturn love sonnet.' We join the folks in the plant (pictures enclosed) in saying . . . 'Enjoy your Saturn, Ms. S!'"

A FINE SON

Just when you need a story one appears!

My son Rodney is perhaps the world's greatest practitioner of servant selling. One day a woman walked into the newly opened Rod's Stereo Sounds, my kiddo's business in Kerrville, Texas. (I'm a pretty proud Dad over the fact that he never took a penny of Mom and Dad's money to open his business. Pretty cool in these days of "let Daddy pick up the tab.")

The woman had $3,500 cash in an envelope and a list of stereo equipment that could outfit a theater. "Can you get me everything on this list for $3,500?" she asked my son.

Rodney looked at the list, did a quick mental calculation, and said, "I think so. This is pretty sophisticated equipment. You must be a serious music lover."

"Actually," said the lady, "this is a list of stereo equipment that my ex-husband left to me. It was damaged by lightning, and this is the insurance money that they gave me to replace it."

Rod asked if, like her ex-husband, she was an audiophile. No, she just listened to the radio and an occasional CD. She was worried about fitting everything into her new but small apartment.

"I can sell you a terrific system for less than half of what you have in that envelope. You don't need all that equipment for your apartment. You can use the rest of the money for something that's more important to you."

What would the average salesperson have done? He probably would have sold her the entire list, and surprise, the total would have been within pennies of $3,500.

"I can't believe you're doing this," said the woman.

"That's because you don't understand how my business works. You see, I give you great equipment at good prices, follow up with a little service, and you tell everybody in town!"

"There's a book out called *Positively Outrageous Service*. My new boss gave it to me to read before starting to work. And I think what you are giving me is what they call POS. I'll bet you've even read the book. The author lives here in the Hill Country. Do you know him?"

(I'll bet you know the next line in this story!)

The first week or so Rodney was in business, a local businessman stopped by the store. "I think my stereo is shot, but since I probably won't keep this car long, I'd like to stay under $500 or $600."

Rodney suggested that the stereo might be fine. It could be the speakers that were the problem. He offered to put in a pair of speakers that he had on sale for $129, saying that if that wasn't the solution, he would remove them at no charge.

The speakers turned out to be the problem, and the customer left ecstatic about having spent far less than the $600 that many salespeople would have found reason to charge.

What makes this story better is that not all that many folks in town are aware that Rodney is my son. Who told me this great story about servant selling? It wasn't Rodney—it was someone who had heard it from someone else who had heard the story.

(Fast-forward ten years.)

I was waiting to get my hair cut, had my nose in my computer and my feet propped up on the glass-topped table near the door, when a light touch on my arm brought me to the moment. It was Helen. Short, blonde, and sweeter than punch, Helen has been a stylist in our little town for years. Everyone knows Helen and just as many think highly of her.

"I've got to tell you what a wonderful job you did raising your son."

My feet popped off the table and I sat up straight. "My son? Rod?"

"Yes, Rod. Do you know what he did for me?"

"I haven't a clue. What?"

I really had no clue. For me it's a bit of a shock to discover that you and your kiddo have friends in common. It's so . . . adult. I hadn't thought until that moment that when the Kiddo was just starting out in his car stereo business, Helen had been working at a small shop next door.

"I went into his store because I needed to replace my TV."

Rod's Stereo Sounds doesn't sell TVs, so I joined the smiling cat in thinking things were getting curiouser and curiouser.

"He drove me to San Antonio to his distributor (at least 120 miles round trip), helped me pick out the TV, sold it to me at cost, delivered it to my house, and then after he finished running his errands, came back and installed it! I told him he didn't have to do that!" I thought I saw the beginning of a tear as she finished the story.

"He said, 'Helen, when I was just starting out you used to send people to my store. We really needed the business back then . . .'

"I told him I was going to tell you about this. Guess you already know what a great guy your son is. You and Melanie should be really proud."

We are.

A MATTER OF INTERPRETATION

It's a scary thing to turn employees loose with little more than a touch of training and a dose of confidence that they will be able to love customers without meeting unintended disaster. It takes a tremendously competent organization to deliver POS.

Yes, you read that right. Positively Outrageous Service follows organizational competence.

Take Southwest Airlines for example. To one large $40 million airplane add 35,000 feet of altitude, about 130 passengers, then stir in a couple of young flight attendants. Tell those flight attendants to "go play with the customers" and see what you get five miles above the earth without a stitch of adult supervision. It's scary, huh?

It takes a competent organization to deliver POS.

And what happens if you take an immature organization and hurry the process. Well, darlin', you're gonna lose more than a few.

Come to think of it, even if yours is a highly competent operation, you're still going to lose one now and again for two reasons. First, you're going to run into the customer that is so used to getting crummy service that, when faced with a playful, loving service person, will misinterpret the attempt and get offended.

I think of the time I was working the drive-thru at the little franchised restaurant that we used to own. A woman pulled to the outdoor menu board, and I went to work.

"Hi, may I serve you?"

"I'm so hungry. What size orders do you have?" (This was a fried chicken franchise.)

"Ma'am, you are in luck. We have a new 100-piece box of chicken called a Crowd Pleaser. How many would you like?"

There was a brief pause before she answered, "That's too big! I'm hungry but not that hungry."

"Just kidding, ma'am. We have a 16-piece, a 12-piece, or an 8-piece whole chicken dinner, any of which should fill you up big time."

"Whoa! That's still too big! I'm hungry but I can't eat a whole chicken for lunch!"

"No problem, ma'am. I have a 3-piece order, a 2-piece chicken dinner, and a 1-piece chicken snack. And if the chicken snack is too big for you, I can take a bite out of it and adjust it to size."

We never saw her again!

3

SAM WALTON'S KILLING ME! *Or Why POS Is the Competitive Advantage*

"Look at the longhorn steer.
When the grass gets short around the water hole, he goes farther out."
GREAT-GRANDPA RHYNE

"There are no low volume locations, just low volume management."
T. SCOTT GROSS

It was a beautiful spring evening as we drove deserted streets past a dozen or more small businesses, some closed early for the evening, some closed forever. At the far end of town, only Wal-Mart could boast a full parking lot. And the scene could have been Anywhere, USA. If it's not a picture of your town, just wait.

The discounters have brought variety and quality at low prices to small town America. Sam Walton can't be held responsible for the resulting deaths of scores of Main Streets. It is true, though, that many would like to lay the blame squarely at his feet.

Sam just had a good idea, first. About half of his detractors must secretly wish that they had had the same idea first—that, plus the guts to do something with it.

Wal-Mart has created quite a stir with its impact on small town America. But that's only because it's easier to spot trends and connect cause with effect in communities that rarely stretch more than a mile or two border to border. Even though small town America has become our laboratory for studying the impact of discounters, it would be foolish to even hint that the same things don't happen in our largest cities.

There are no cities—just clusters of small towns. For most retailers, if the edge of the world were suddenly moved to within a two-mile radius of their store, it would be up to CNN to let them know, because the impact at the cash register would be negligible.

If it hadn't been Sam Walton who spotted the need for variety, quality, and value, it would have been someone else who would be labeled the despot of Main Street. Even in small towns, individual tragedy is too easily overlooked when the community is apparently benefiting from a trend that brings toasters and microwaves for the first time to lower and middle-class homes.

Besides, a toaster is easier to notice once it's sitting on your counter than in old man Smith's now closed variety store. And wasn't he about to retire anyway?

In the larger sense, the Smiths of Anytown have been edged out by the quick-witted marketing savvy of Sam Walton and others. But it hasn't really been a case of sophisticated city slicker MBAs knocking off well-meaning but ill-equipped small business people. Too often the little guy has cried foul, when the truth could be more easily found in the mirror.

It's not fair to call the casualties of retailing crybabies. Most fought bravely and didn't quit until well after the battle was lost. They are guilty of fighting poorly.

The following is an article from a small town Texas newspaper. The names have been changed, just because:

Unfavorable Conditions Cited Reason for Selling

Charlie Smith owned and operated a local business for 15 years but was forced to sell out to a major chain for various reasons that revolve around what he feels were unfavorable economic conditions.

Smith's opened in 1973 and was experiencing 12 to 24 percent increases every year up to 1986, Smith explained.

He felt the business was a successful one to that point.

In 1985 the small business had its best year ever with sales totals exceeding $750,000.

"Gross profits were good and net profits were good," Smith explained.

This banner year and the 12 previous years gave Smith the idea of expanding and investing in an attempt to instigate a growth pattern.

It was at this point that trouble began, according to Smith.

He went to the bank and borrowed money to invest in his business. Remodeling was done and new equipment was added to the existing stock.

"We had no reason to think that the economy would fall apart in 1986," he added.

Smith researched before committing to such a large investment. He found that the interest rate was favorable, unemployment was down, the Gross National Product was stable, and inflation was down.

"We could only assume, because of sales, we would do well because of the stats and our previous sales," continued Smith.

He said the Anytown Area Chamber of Commerce might be at fault in a sense.

"They play a numbers game," he explained. "It's their job to make the numbers look good regardless of what they actually are.

"I am not denying the fact that the figures are factual the way they present them. However, they play with the numbers until they appear positive.

"I know because I have played the game," he said alluding to the time that he spent on the board of directors for the Chamber.

Another large factor for the loss of Smith's was the opening of Wal-Mart four years ago.

Smith explained that Wal-Mart carries "quick-moving items" that appeal to many buyers.

In an attempt to keep people buying locally, Smith kept many of the slower-moving items in stock.

"Things people need very seldom," Smith explained.

The quick-moving items are the cream of the crop, according to Smith. And once he started losing his normal sales, he was forced to stop stocking the slower-moving items.

"In most areas we were always competitive with Wal-Mart and our service ability helped us," continued Smith.

"After surviving Kmart's invasion into the area, it was difficult to come out on top with Wal-Mart," he said.

There is only a certain amount of available monies in the area and when you are forced to split them three ways in an economically trying time, you will not win, Smith explained.

It was early in 1987 that Smith and his family realized that they were not going to make it.

He tried once again to borrow money from a financial institution in an effort to stay on his feet until the "depression" was over, he said.

"We had adjusted out all variables in our outgoing money," Smith said. "All businesses have to look to lending institutions when times are bad.

"When the lending institutions will no longer support you in your efforts to regain stability, this is what happens."

Smith sold his business to his franchisor.

"I sold out under duress and paid everybody I owed," he said. Smith said he would go back into business tomorrow if he had private investors and did not have to borrow from an Anytown lending institution.

Smith is a nice man, the kind of man you would want for a neighbor, mayor, or favorite uncle. But nice or not, look again at the article and see who he thinks is to blame. He blames Kmart, Wal-Mart, the economy, and finally the local bank for not supporting an obviously failing business.

At least he had the good grace not to blame his neighbors for shopping with the competition. In that respect, Smith is an exception. In small towns everywhere, consumers are being berated for not keeping their dollars local. Running into a friend at a nearby big city mall is like meeting your preacher at a topless bar. You both hope you won't be recognized, and if a meeting can't be avoided, you both blubber out some lame excuse for existing!

Smith was a brave soldier and a dead one. He didn't understand the uncomplicated concepts behind the Four Wall Marketing Theory. Neither did the hero of "The Painted Window Story."

THE PAINTED WINDOW STORY

The intersection was just west of Boston, too far from town to be called a suburb but too close to be considered a part of Boston. Some 300 feet from the corner sat an A&W Root Beer restaurant. You remember A&W, don't you?

At one time the A&W family consisted of nearly 2,500 mostly ma-and-pa operations scattered across America with a smattering of foreign operations. A&W is the restaurant chain that should have been McDonald's. They were there first, often in the best location, and frequently without competition.

But A&W either wouldn't or couldn't change. It failed to recognize and respond to a changing consumer. Up until recently, A&W was but a shell of its former self. The new owner, Yum Foods, knew how to fix that!

It was the lunch hour when the young A&W field rep walked into the restaurant. He had noticed that weeds were growing through the cracks in the parking lot, and that the light standards had begun to rust. Inside, the few tables that had been occupied by the sparse lunch crowd were still dirty. Crew members were out of uniform. A radio was blaring.

The owner, known for his love of fishing, was resting feet up, tying a fishing lure. He stared out the window at the new, sparkling clean, and very busy McDonald's that had been built smack on the corner.

Without shifting his gaze, the owner said, "That damned McDonald's is killing me! Ever since they opened that damned place, my sales have gone straight into the dumper! If you think you're going to continue collecting royalties from me, you'd better get off your backside and help me out!"

"No problem," replied the youngster.

With that, he quietly let himself out of the office. In about 20 minutes, he returned carrying a small brown bag.

"Here, this might be just what you need to turn the corner."

"What's this for?" asked the owner as he removed a very small can of black paint and a small, inexpensive brush. "What am I supposed to do with this?"

"Paint that window black," risked the field rep. "And I think you'll have less trouble with McDonald's. Judging from the looks of your parking lot, dining room, and employees, my guess is that McDonald's has done more than attract the attention of your customers. It looks like they attracted your attention as well. It looks to me as if they're paying more attention to your customers than you are," he continued.

"Get out!" was the owner's reply.

The field man left. But it was the owner who got out. Permanently.

P O S   P o i n t

There are no low volume locations, only low volume managers.

FOUR WALL MARKETING

The idea isn't new. Neither is the terminology. Unfortunately for all of our sophistication, we have somehow forgotten that ultimately our marketing strategies live or die within our own four walls.

In simpler times when our competitors were unable to reach out and entice our customers with an electronic message, people understood intuitively that taking care of business meant taking care of the customer. And that, of course, meant making certain that whatever transpired within our own four walls had to be perfect.

When populations are spread thinly marketing loses its meaning. Competitors are so far apart that marketing loses its meaning. It just isn't convenient to travel long distances for small savings on life's necessities. Marketing only makes sense when your competitor locates within easy traveling distance to your customers. It makes even more sense when your competition sets up shop right next door.

Still, marketing only begets trial. It is the daily, one-on-one activity that occurs inside your own four walls that creates compelling word of mouth and repeat business.

Few businesses can survive by serving a customer only once and then looking for another new customer to take her place. Four Wall Marketing is whatever you do that turns customers into friends. Four Wall Marketing can mean a revival of the new-old techniques of serving outrageously.

HOW TO FIND OUT WHAT CUSTOMERS REALLY WANT

The cake was grand. Smothered in cherry topping and wrapped in a thick cream frosting, it was a birthday surprise. When the office finally cleared, one little piece was left to carry home to my wife.

Not surprising, when it was her birthday she asked for a cake just like the one they served at my office celebration. The problem was it had been home-baked by a temporary worker who we couldn't locate.

No problem. I'll call the bakery, describe the cake, and who will be the wiser?

"Hello. I'd like to order a yellow sheet cake with cherry topping, kinda like what you would find in a cherry pie. And can you put a cream frosting on the sides and perhaps in a lattice pattern across the top?"

"I'm sorry. We don't have a cake like that."

"Well, it's fine with me if we don't get it exact. But could you try please?"

"It's not in our book."

"Yes, ma'am, I understand that. I was just hoping that I could describe the cake, and you would bake it for me."

"I wouldn't know what to charge."

"Well, charge me whatever you think is fair and then add $5 for your trouble, just to make sure you come out all right."

"I can't. If it's not in our book, we can't bake it."

"Do you bake yellow sheet cakes?"

"Yes, that's a number four."

"Do you bake cherry pies?"

"Yes, that's a number 17."

"Great! Bake me a yellow sheet cake and a cherry pie, but before you put them into boxes, scoop the pie filling onto the cake."

"That's not in our book, sir."

True story.

Here's one with a happy ending at McGuffey's Restaurants in Asheville, North Carolina. A family entered one of McGuffey's units with a very unhappy child in tow. It seems that the kiddo had his heart set on eating at McDonald's. When the news of the unhappy diner reached the kitchen manager, an employee was immediately dispatched to a nearby McDonald's and within minutes delivered a Big Mac to the surprised child.

Serving the customer what he or she wants may not be found in everyone's book. But at McGuffey's, it's on page one!

The whole of business is finding a need and filling it. And you can't fill a need unless you know about it. Any business that doesn't have a system for customer feedback is a solution looking for a problem.

In our own business, our number-one rule is: Always try to say yes to a customer. Say no when it's for his or her own good.

Carl Sewell in *Customers for Life* (Doubleday, 1990) put it like this: "When the customer asks, the answer is always yes. Period."

That's a pretty firm position, but only if you know what the customer wants. You would think that customers would come right out and tell you what they want. It seems so obvious. In fact, customers don't always tell you what they want, particularly if what they have is a complaint. Complaints are requests to get it right, to keep your promise.

Every sale carries with it a promise. With service, the promise is often only implied.

For $14.95 you get a 14-ounce T-bone cooked to order with choice of potato, fresh vegetables, and garden salad. Appetizers, drinks, and desserts are not included. Read the menu, dummy! It's all there in black and white!

On the other hand, convenient parking, clean restrooms, comfortable smoke-free surroundings, pleasant greetings, and efficient friendly service—that's all implied. Part of the cost, of course!

The same is true for any other purchase. A new computer comes with power cord, monitor, manual, and system software. It's all listed on the box. But can I call you if there's a problem? How many times? Will you be able to assist? Will you *want* to assist? All this is implied.

That's a funny thing about service. It's a major portion of product cost but rarely mentioned on the packaging.

You would think that customers cheated out of their service would complain. According to the U.S. Office of Consumer Affairs, between 37 and 45 percent of consumers who are unhappy with service, do not complain. They go elsewhere.

They may go elsewhere, but they never forget. And when they remember you, it's always with the kind of word of mouth that causes you to die a thousand deaths, once from embarrassment and 999 times at the cash register as would-be customers get the message. They join the one dissatisfied customer as they "vote with their feet and cross the street."

We mentioned earlier that the definition of Positively Outrageous Service is more than an outline of the best service you ever experienced. It also defines your worst service experience. When you talk with someone about a POS experience, they are usually chomping at the bit for you to finish so they can tell a story of their own. This is also true when it's a story of outrageously poor service.

Outrageously poor service, like its upbeat cousin Positively Outrageous Service, is also:

- Random and unexpected
- Out of proportion to the circumstance
- Highly personal to the customer

And it, too, creates:

- Compelling word of mouth
- Lifetime buying decisions

For this reason, *every* business needs a customer service feedback system. Call it damage control if you wish, or just call it enlightened business acumen. But have one you must.

According to Patricia Sellers's article in *Fortune* magazine, there is a surprising payoff for those companies that make a science of listening to the customer.

"When they make their customers happy, they make their employees happy, too. Contented workers make for better-served customers. And there is also mounting evidence that improvement in customer satisfaction leads directly to higher employee retention."

In the end, nearly everyone is a customer. Particularly in a tight labor market, businesses hope to market their package of wages, benefits, and working conditions to employees. After all, what is retention other than an expression of an employee's feelings about the value he or she received in return for an investment of time and energy?

As long as we're being enlightened, we may as well include your suppliers in the same package. Suppliers stop at many other doors before and after you. They can provide marketing and product development insights, price breaks, delivery, and billing flexibility. And some even provide their customers with management development. Treated properly, a supplier can be a major asset.

Wise is the one who listens; for in the end, we all are customers. In the end, we all vote with our pocketbooks and with our efforts. And in the end, it is the one who listens that includes us, empowers us, and wins our loyalty.

CUSTOMER FEEDBACK SYSTEMS

Only in business heaven is every employee a "10 percenter." (Coming up in Chapter 12.) For those operating in the real world who cannot handle every customer personally, a customer feedback system is just what the doctor ordered.

When handled properly, comment cards can become an excellent marketing tool. But the operating word is *properly*.

There are four components of a properly handled customer feedback system: it should be immediate, top level, sensitive, and must extend an offer.

To respond immediately, you must have the customer's name, address, and phone number. A serious complaint deserves more than a follow-up letter; it deserves a personal phone call.

Complaining customers are looking for a resolution of what they see as a conflict. They may want something fixed, an apology after slow service, or restitution for missing, damaged, or shoddy products. They want justice, and justice delayed really is justice denied. Besides, every hour that you delay in setting things right is another hour for the customer to stew in his or her anger and another opportunity to tell someone else about how awful he or she has been treated. Worse, a delayed response says, "We don't care."

Communication to customers should be immediate and from someone with at least an impressive title. Both the quick response and the high-level respondent tell the customer that he or she is important. A sensitive response with a promise to take action tells customers that you really listened.

Nearly every response should extend an offer of either a thank-you for suggestions or compensation for slights, real or imagined.

Here are some simple suggestions:

- *Sample your product.* Occasionally ask your customers to "try on" your product. Let them have a taste, a test drive, or some other small sample of your product and service in exchange for answering a few questions. Your customers will be delighted to help, and they will revel in the opportunity to be heard and have an impact on your business.
- *Include customer comment cards with every order.* At least occasionally include a customer comment card with every order and make certain that they are conveniently available 100 percent of the time.
- *Post a direct phone number.* Post the direct phone number of the manager or owner where customers can find it easily. The owner's home number is best, and you will be surprised to find that most customers will respect your privacy except in the most desperate instance, in which case you will want to be disturbed.

  (We had our home number posted on the menu board at our last restaurant and only received two phone calls in the eight years we operated the restaurant. The first was from a customer, who hung up without telling us on discovering that he was calling our home and deciding that his complaint was too small to bother us at home! And the second was after we no longer owned the store! So, yes, we will again have our number available on the printed menu at our new restaurant. How else can we prove that we are quality fanatics?)

- *Call the customer.* Whenever you can, without inconvenience to the customer, get a phone number. On a random basis, call and find out how you are doing. Most customers will be so delighted that you cared enough to call they won't mind the interruption. When you call, know exactly what the customer purchased and when. This act alone qualifies as Positively Outrageous Service. It is random and unexpected. It is out of proportion to the circumstance, or at least it is out of the norm. The customer, of course, is highly involved, invited to share something very personal—an opinion!

Most service calls should be made by someone as high up the corporate ladder as possible. At least have someone say "I'm calling on behalf of our owner" or some such status-bequeathing phrase.

No doubt compelling word of mouth will result. "I got the nicest call. Yes, the owner of Acme called just to check up on service. What a nice person!"

And of course such a call could contribute to lifetime buying decisions. Who wouldn't want to do business with someone who cares enough to consult you after the sale?

WHILE CUSTOMERS ARE WAITING, SERVE THEM OUTRAGEOUSLY

There is no greater opportunity to offend a customer or poorly treat a customer than a line. Customers usually hate waiting in lines, but it doesn't have to be this way. Understand the psychology of lines, and it's simple science to turn a line into a competitive advantage.

Here are the facts about lines:

Lines are self-limiting. There is a point at which people will no longer join a line. That point is determined solely by the perceived value of what is at the end of the line compared with the value of the line member's time.

Let's say there is a line, and at the end of this line are crisp $1 bills. Each time you get to the head of the line, you receive a single bill. How long would you wait in this line? If you would wait for five minutes, you value your time at $12 per hour. Would you wait an hour? And what if the reward was a crisp $100 bill?

People will join lines that stretch for blocks to board a spectacular Disney ride or attraction. They wouldn't normally join a similar line to purchase a hamburger. Obviously, many facts influence the perceived value of joining a line. How hungry you are for food or entertainment could have a dramatic impact on your willingness to wait. If your line is long, your sales will be short.

Lines can form only when customers arrive faster than they can be served. Think about it. If a customer comes in and is served before the next customer comes in, you cannot have a line. A line is possible only if a second customer arrives while the first customer is waiting for service to complete the transaction. Every time you see a line, you can be absolutely certain that at one time customers were arriving faster than they were being served.

Airlines and banks know about lines. Unfortunately, they don't know quite enough, because they add extra service only *after* a line begins to form. If they have enough employees available to keep the line from growing, then they have enough available to have kept a line from forming in the first place.

Lines once formed persist indefinitely. In the case of banks or airlines, notice that as long as management exactly balances the ability of the system to serve against the speed of arrival of new customers the line will continue to persist indefinitely. It cannot shrink, because whenever a customer is served a new customer takes her place. Whether the line is 2 or 102 customers long, it will never change its size.

Once service is delayed for any reason, every subsequent customer will wait for the length of the original delay. If ever there was an argument for original sin, this is it. Let's say the world is unfolding perfectly. Every 60 seconds a new face walks in the door, makes a purchase, and turns to leave just in time to smile at the next customer. Now imagine what happens if you run out of merchandise and have to race to the stockroom, a round-trip that takes two minutes.

Something is different, out of place when you return to the sales floor. Now instead of one customer there are two. Try as you might, you can only serve one customer per minute. Just as you bid one good afternoon, another customer steps into line behind the one waiting customer. You are doomed forever to face a line.

The interesting effect is that every subsequent customer must wait the two minutes you spent running to the stockroom. Theoretically, this would continue forever, each customer paying in turn the price of your original sin.

Lines are only as long as they appear. People do not study lines. They take a quick look and make an instant decision. That's why you see snaking lines at Wendy's, and you don't see them at McDonald's.

Snaked lines are shorter than straight lines, at least that is the customer's perception. In the early 1970s, a major quick-service restaurant company developed what many thought was the world's most labor-efficient kitchen layout, capable of serving hundreds of customers an hour and requiring only a sparse crew of employees. The design met all of its creative specs except one. The customers hated it.

Customers were lined up in a single straight file. Even though the line moved very quickly, potential customers would see the one long line and instantly decide that, based on their experiences with quick-service restaurants, there was no way they could expect to be served from a line like that in less than six months! The design was abandoned.

McDonald's seems to understand that a customer would rather be number three in a slow-moving line than number nine in a fast line. Service always occurs in the customer's mind.

Here's where Positively Outrageous Service, or more specifically showmanship, can make all the difference.

WAIT NOT, WANT NOT

Making a wait pleasant or at least bearable requires a little creativity and just a touch of generosity. Just be careful not to do it second rate. Think about the last time you waited in some dingy auto repair shop, drinking stale coffee, smelling like old smoke, and reading even older magazines. In most cases, no waiting area would be a better plan.

Here are a few examples of people who do it right:

- *Southwest Airlines.* They provide hot coffee for their customers in the boarding area for sleepy-eyed commuter flights. And most Southwest gate areas are equipped with televisions to help you pass the time and keep current with the news or afternoon soaps.
- *The Olive Garden.* Waiting at the Olive Garden is almost as good as the meal. You get to people-watch while friendly employees circulate with baskets of straight-from-the-oven breadsticks . . . mmm.
- *Marriott.* Probably the best at paying attention to waiting customers, called "guests," Marriott is quick to offer juice or fresh fruit to guests waiting to check in or out.

- *Krispy Kreme Doughnuts.* Pop into a Krispy Kreme Doughnut shop when they're busy and you'll find they're never too busy to offer a hot, delicious doughnut right off the conveyor belt straight to your mouth—while you wait!

BECOME A PRODUCT AND SERVICE FANATIC

Nothing tells the customer that he or she is important like being fanatical over getting the product, service, and order perfect.

In addition to making the customer happy, true quality fanaticism creates legends. That's the compelling word of mouth that makes service that is truly positively outrageous.

Everyone has heard the story about the FedEx driver who wrestled the entire drop box into his truck when he couldn't find the key and didn't want the packages to miss the flight. (That story came from one of Tom Peter's books, along with the story of the night janitor at a Domino's Pizza warehouse who braved heavy weather and the potential wrath of his supervisor when he left the job to deliver pizza dough to a unit that otherwise would have run out.)

Don't be intimidated by these stories. Settle for the title of "ordinary fanatic"! You don't have to be faster than a speeding bullet or able to leap tall buildings in a single bound. You only have to care. And caring pays off.

We were in Bandera, Texas, having dinner with our son and family when he recognized the waitress as one of his newest customers. (Rod owns Rod's Stereo Sounds in Kerrville, about 20 miles from Bandera, and he never forgets a customer!)

He asked her how she was enjoying her new radio that was installed in her car.

"I love it, but when I crank the volume way, way up, the speakers cut out."

"Well, that's not okay."

"I guess that I just shouldn't be doing that, so it's not a big deal."

"It sure is! That's not supposed to happen. Why don't you bring it in tomorrow and let us get that right for you. When we check it out, you'll be able to crank it up as much as you like. Can you bring it in in the morning?"

She did. And he did. And the world was right again.

4

SERVICE IS AN AFFAIR
OF THE HEART

Human nature is not likely to change. People will always do business with people they like, but the context will change dramatically. Technology will be an influence, but buying will remain a matter of what, or more likely who, makes me feel good. A great example of how the context changes but the motivators do not can be found on the Internet. Click to http://www.landsend .com, a great Web site with lots of helpful features.

But guess which one is really taking off? Live chat! So we don't want to call in our order, but once we're online, now we can talk. People like to buy from people, and they like to buy from people they like. Decisions will continue to be made on a feel-good, don't-want-to-feel-bad basis.

We have a backup GPS unit in our airplane made by Garmin. After years of faithful service, the display went on the fritz and the bracket on the now-discontinued model also headed south. So I called Garmin, immediately got connected to a friendly guy named Scott, and told him my problem.

After listening to me describe the problem, he said, "I think the problem is with your backup battery."

"I looked for that and couldn't find it anywhere. Tell me where it is and I'll replace it."

"Unfortunately, on those early models the backup battery is soldered to the board. It's a factory-only repair, but if you will send it in we'll replace it no charge. While we have it we'll give you a free database update. And, come to think of it, I know we don't have any mounting brackets in stock, but if you don't mind getting one that was used on a training unit, I have one here in my office I can give you."

Deal! So guess what equipment I'll be ordering when the old GPS finally bites the dust?

SERVICE AS AN EXPERIENCE

Once we have separated service from the hard product, we are left with two components: commodity and experience. Folks who do not do a good job of customer service will want to disguise it, so that the commodity and the experience are inseparable. Others will deal strictly on price. For this group, the challenge will be to keep the customer from knowing too much about the product. We see this today as manufacturers build one item but tag it with multiple model numbers for the sole intention of making it impossible to comparison shop.

The last group will be those folks who efficiently produce an outstanding service product and are not too proud to put a visible price tag on it.

MBWA—Tom Peters Said It!

Can't you see some starch-shirted manager wringing his hands while pondering the question, "How can we find out what the customer really wants?" Think about it. There he sits in a plush office somewhere deep in the halls of the Puzzle Palace hoping for divine intervention with a problem the receptionist could solve between calls. Ask them!

Tom Peters helped popularize the concept of MBWA (management by walking around) in his book *In Search of Excellence* (Harper & Row, 1982). It's such an obvious concept that it's embarrassing. Still, we get so hung up in technology, psychology, and demography that we forget the best way to find out what our customers want is to *ask*.

James "Buddy" Parker used to say that comfortable offices and pagers were two things that effective managers would never need. "Gives them an excuse to be someplace they aren't supposed to be," he said, on many occasions. This was in the days before cell phones. Oh, he would have loved cell phones!

If your job was to serve the customers or support those who did, then Buddy couldn't figure what use an office could be. It should, he figured, be just large enough to accommodate a safe, one chair, and an adding machine. More than that and you would be cheating the shareholders by squandering their assets—and cheating customers by denying them your attention.

Pagers fell into Buddy's same dark category. If you were supposed to be in the store, then why would you need a pager? If you couldn't be easily found, then you would be out of place. Period.

Whether it's Peters or Parker, the place for management is with the customer, guest, patron, or member. And the higher up the ladder, the *more* visible you should be. After all, beyond a quality product, what can we give the customer? Quality service, of course! What is not so obvious is that a major component of service is status.

I'd Rather Meet a Dumb Owner . . .

Stephen Michaelides, the editor of *Restaurant Business,* once wrote an interesting comment that a customer would rather meet a dumb owner than a sharp manager. What he meant was that since status is such an important component of customer service, the very fact that the owner—make that OWNER—takes a personal interest in the guest (customer), more status is conferred.

He did not say that it's okay to hire stupid managers! What is true is that the higher an individual resides in the corporate hierarchy the greater the impact of direct customer contact. People revel in their stories about being greeted or treated by the owner. "The owner came out and introduced herself." "The owner took us on a private tour of the facility."

Excellent or perhaps just "good" service delivered by the owner, president, or grand pooh-bah takes on outrageous proportions, simply because each one adds personal status to the event.

WOO!

Donald Clifton, president and CEO of Selection Research, Inc., offers an interesting customer-based method of evaluating your business. Clifton's measuring sticks are *awareness, preference, frequency,* and *relationship extension.*

Awareness is expressed as the percentage of the potential market that is aware of your operation. Aware customers or potential customers would be those who know your location, perhaps hours of operation, and have a general knowledge of your products and services.

Preference is expressed as the percentage of your market base that given a choice would prefer your product or service over that of the competition.

Here's where Clifton's measurements get interesting. Frequency is the number of visits or purchases per month or year or whatever. Relationship extension is reflected in the percentage of your customers who feel as though they are recognized as individuals. Being called by name is probably the most important indicator, but it's not the only one. "Good morning, Mrs. Tate," may be perfect, but "Hi! I haven't seen you in awhile" certainly runs a close second.

What is interesting is how frequency and relationship extension relate. Quite simply, the more you extend a personal relationship to your customers, the more likely it will be that they will increase their patronage. Theoretically, it's possible to double your sales without adding a single new customer. All that must be done is to make your current customers feel so good about doing business with you that they come in twice as often.

Impossible? Not at all! One week in our former fried chicken franchise restaurant sales were up 82.6 percent over the same week the previous year, with only a minor increase in sales per transaction. Most of that increase was due solely to higher customer counts. And the town was not one iota larger or richer. Something changed, and that something happened within our own four walls. It's called better service.

Relationship extension is Don Clifton's term. I call it *feel good*.

Feel good. That's just another name for status. And who can give the customer the most status? Why the owner, of course!

It's not possible in most businesses for the owner to meet and greet every customer. Most customers don't expect such attention. They do appreciate the owner's presence. Having the owner on hand usually conveys a certain sense of security that the product or service will be done right. And if there is a problem, the owner is at least available.

One of Clifton's other terms is *WOO*. For those instances when a customer must be handled by an employee, Clifton says the magic word is WOO. WOO is that touchy-feely personality trait that allows employees to reach out and in a matter of a few seconds, extend a little feel good to the customer. WOO unfortunately is not an easily trainable talent. You either have it or you don't.

Employees with WOO—we call them Service Naturals—are the best customer feedback system possible. Service Naturals listen and respond instantly to the customers' needs. They make thousands of operational adjustments every day, as they ride the ebb and flow of individual customers' emotional needs.

The trends are unmistakable. Success will belong to those who are best at honoring the oldest traditions of customer service—just lovin' on customers.

Listen to your customers, give them exactly what they want—any way they want it—and invite them in to participate in their own service. This will be the new-old way of succeeding, an announcement of a return to the days when the customer was both friend and neighbor. Now there's a concept that's positively outrageous!

SUPPORT CAUSES THE CUSTOMER HOLDS AS IMPORTANT

When we opened our restaurant in a community that was new to us, we asked the banker, contractor, and city officials what charity organization had the widest support of the community. "Hospice" was the most common response. So we took the cue and held a preopening party, as a training exercise, and suggested that attendees donate the menu price of their meal to the hospice. Neither the community nor the hospice has forgotten.

Robert Love was a regular customer. We discovered that his grandmother was in the hospital (and she loved our food!).

"How's Grandma's appetite?" we asked.

"Fine. She gets out tomorrow and wants to stop here on the way home!"

We didn't think Grandma should have to wait, and minutes later, her meal was delivered—on the house, of course.

You can't support every cause, so choose causes that have high visibility among your customer base. And when you support a cause, give it more than lip service. Support it with your time, talent, and dollars. Your customers will notice and come to the cash register to thank you personally.

It is surprising what will grab the attention of your customers. Things you do that you think are above and beyond may get little notice. Sometimes, things that you do in the normal course of business will turn out to be surprise hits with your customers.

We decided that our dining area wasn't getting the attention it needed. We were getting too busy to love on our customers and keep the area looking its best. When you are too busy to love on the customers, you are too darned busy. Your unloved customers will help you get things back in balance by staying away, so that you'll have fewer customers to worry over.

Our solution was to find a learning-disabled person and train her as a dining room attendant. We looked for the friendliest, most-loving individual we could find. We gave little weight to experience and possible ability to perform tasks beyond routine cleaning. Instead, we told our gal that her main job was to make absolutely certain that every customer was made to feel as if they were a guest in her home.

Did it work? You bet!

Three quarters of all customer comment cards mentioned our dining room attendant by name. Many said that she was the reason we got their business. And of course, our regulars were often greeted with more than a smile—they got a hug.

Support causes that are important to your customers and be willing to be surprised at what really turns them on.

SAY YOU'RE SORRY FOR THE SLIGHTEST SLIP FROM YOUR STANDARD

When our customers had to wait more than one minute for their food to cook, we offered a courtesy drink. This small apology helped make the wait more pleasant. It also told the customer that we were serious about our business and valued their time.

The Positively Outrageous Service Rules for Apology

- When in doubt—apologize.
- Apologize even when the customer doesn't know you goofed.
- Always make amends in excess of the slipup.
- Empower everyone to solve problems.
- Handle mistakes by the numbers.

When in doubt—apologize. The idea of being right has little value to the outrageous server. If the customer perceives a slight or a mistake, forget about being right. The customer is right.

Take your lumps, apologize, and waste absolutely no time explaining why things happened the way they did. Apologize, make amends, explain what you will do to prevent future occurrences, and apologize again.

Apologize even when the customer doesn't know you goofed. An unexpected apology has such positive and lasting impact that it is almost worth creating situations that you can use. Dropping in an extra biscuit, saying "You waited just a little too long to suit us, so here's a biscuit to munch on the way home," is such a pleasant surprise. This is especially true when the customer didn't think the wait was too long anyway.

A dry cleaner can pin on a small mending kit and say "I really wanted to have this for you yesterday." An auto dealer can say "One of our mechanics leaned against the fender and smudged it a bit, so we had your car washed and waxed to make up for it."

We routinely apologized to customers who waited for more than a second or two in our drive-thru. "Sorry to keep you waiting" was a favorite line, especially when we'd say it just as the customer rolled down the window. Sometimes we'd say, "Hi! I'll be back with you in a New York second." And then only a few seconds later we'd say, "Thanks for being patient. Are you ready to order?"

And the customer thinks, "If they apologize for service like this, I don't think I could handle what they call really good service."

Mike Bates of the Widman Popcorn Company was enjoying lunch with a friend at a Red Lobster Restaurant. According to Mike, the service was friendly and fast and the food right on target. Imagine his surprise when the manager approached the table and explained that, because it took 11 minutes rather than the promised 10, the entire meal would be on the house. Now guess who is one of Red Lobster's most loyal customers? And all for the price of lunch!

Always make amends in excess of the slipup. An apology should be so out of proportion to the offense that the customer feels absolutely overwhelmed.

I was introduced to a fellow customer while at our local computer store and told him that he looked familiar. "I think you were at our place for lunch today." He said that it had been the day before and that he really enjoyed the restaurant. When I asked him why, his answer made me uncomfortable at first. After thinking about it, it was quite a compliment.

"We get lunch for the office pretty regularly, and over the years on two occasions our order was completely confused. It's possible that it was our fault, but the result was the same—a messed-up order."

"And that's why you like us?" I was beginning to think this guy was a little kinky!

"Of course not. It's just that when it happened, you people went absolutely overboard to set things right. No one likes to get a screwed-up order, but it's nice to know that if it isn't just perfect you will make a major production out of getting it right."

If you forget to include a biscuit send a coupon good for dinner. If you can't seat them together in coach, bring them to first class. If you can't deliver in time, throw in something extra and don't be stingy.

When you say you are sorry, be so generous that there is no doubt you mean it. You will create so much positive word of mouth that your mistake will be worth its weight in gold. An occasional screwup handled outrageously may be just what the promo doctor ordered!

Empower everyone to solve problems. Larry Okonek, the director of training for PFM, a contract food-service company, likes to snack. He also travels quite a bit. He may be a good trainer, but he is a bit forgetful when it comes to packing for trips. That's how he came to be in search of snack foods and socks while on a business trip to Texas.

He stopped at a chain discount store and in a few minutes found two pairs of identical socks. He seemed destined for a quick in and out. He was a little concerned to find only two of more than a dozen registers open, but no problem, the store wasn't very busy.

Then it happened.

The first pair of socks sailed across the scanner as the UPC bar code was read and the amount recorded. The second identical pair (you guessed it) had no label. Then came the two most-hated words in all of retailing. A voice that would wake the dead screeched "Price check!" over the PA system.

Larry pointed out that the second pair was identical to the first. No deal. Bar code or not, orders are orders.

The natives in line behind Larry became restless. Larry shifted from foot to foot. A native suggested that one pair of socks might be enough for a stranger just passing through town.

Larry considered. It's one thing to stand on principle; it's quite another to stand on principle in dirty socks.

Just when the situation looked as if it would deteriorate into physical violence, a scrawny kid with terminal zits appeared at the register and, yep, sure enough, same price as the first pair.

Larry was out the door before Miss Rocket Science could say, "Thank you for shopping at . . . "

Across the street stood a bright, gleaming beacon in the Texas night, a Kroger supermarket.

Larry stopped and shopped, filling a tote basket with crackers, fruit, and cheese. He fell into line at the express checkout. Home free, almost, until the friendly cashier noticed that the cheese did not have a price tag.

Larry considered running. But before he could complete the thought, the cashier asked, "Did you happen to notice the price?"

"Two forty-nine, I think," offered Larry.

"I didn't think it was that high." She smiled. "I can call for a price check if you like. But would you like to take a chance that two dollars is about right?"

Imagine that! Someone had hired a cashier with brains and then actually had given her the authority to use them.

This is a quiz: Where do you think Larry shops when he needs snacks? Kroger, of course. And what's even better is that they even sell socks!

Handle mistakes by the numbers. Having a system to handle mistakes is somewhat dangerous, because it institutionalizes screwups. It may be saying, "We make so many mistakes that, rather than going to the root of the problem and seeking a solution, we just get better at fixing things."

Customers really are rather forgiving—once. But who would want to patronize a business that had to make mistake-fixing a science.

We received an interesting printed card from one of our very slow-paying clients that read something like this: "Vendors who do not receive payment within 60 days or who receive incorrect payment are invited to call our new problem-resolution line. Please leave a message and a problem-resolution clerk will get back to you within 48 hours."

We had a better way to resolve our problems with this client. We stopped doing business with them. Instead of fixing their system, they developed another system. How much faith could you have in this vendor's ability to resolve problems?

Still, you should have a system for resolving problems and responding to complaints, one that will focus on both resolving the immediate problem and preventing a future occurrence.

Every problem should belong to two people: the person directly responsible and someone with at least an impressive weight-carrying title, preferably the owner.

When you know that problems you've created will come back to haunt you personally, you develop a totally different perspective on quality. This is particularly true when you know that both you and the boss will be charged with setting things right. Involving the boss in setting things right has several benefits:

- It lets the employee know that getting things right is important.
- It lets the customer know that getting things right is important.
- It lets the boss know about problems, so that he or she can focus attention and resources on prevention.

Every problem or complaint should be documented, resolved, and, just to be sure, followed up.

Outrageous
Service is a special joy
Not just a job to do.
At least that's the way it's meant to be
So say those folks with WOO.

Loving on customers can be a chore
Or a privilege . . . it depends
On who's the server, who's the guest,
And the messages we send.

The best kind of service ever given
Is random . . . unexpected.
If you're kind of crazy, you're just right.
In fact, you've been elected.

POS is the kind of thing
That once started gets contagious.
And that's the part that makes work fun
when service gets outrageous!

TRENDS

The big fish do eat the little fish. That's the way it has always been. Still, there are little fish.

Even the big fish worry constantly about some bigger fish swimming around some dark corner. So if even the big fish aren't safe, what's a little guy to do?

The problem isn't what size fish you are; it's what *kind* of fish you are that counts. Little fish don't get eaten simply because they are little. It's more a matter of being in the wrong place at the wrong time.

Today's giant discounters are worried about category killers, mega-operations that focus tightly on a single product category such as toys or office supplies. It's not unusual for the sales of entire product categories to be decimated when a category killer decides to open in close proximity to a discounter.

Category killers have such enormous buying power that they can purchase in truckload quantities for factory-direct delivery. Even the Wal-Marts, Kmarts, Sears, and others don't usually have the volume to individually require truckload orders from a single manufacturer.

Truly, in retail, when it comes to being price competitive, the only thing that counts is distribution. Every time you hear the sound of air brakes at someone's dock, listen closely for the sound of prices going up.

The point is this: If you're a little fish, don't even dream of beating 'em on price. Service—Positively Outrageous Service—is the advantage that belongs to the littlest, most-responsive fish. Little fish that serve outrageously swim rings around the competition.

THE ANSWER, MY FRIENDS, IS BLOWING IN THE TRENDS

The little guy can't compete on price, and discounters are devouring the American market. That's hardly encouragement to the millions of businesses in America with ten or fewer employees. Or is it?

Actually, several trends in America are working to the distinct advantage of those small businesses with the foresight to act rather than react. All of these trends put a premium on participative service.

If Positively Outrageous Service is the epitome of participative service, then those businesses that serve outrageously will enjoy a distinct competitive advantage.

We're in a Fine Mess, Ollie

Let's look into the crystal ball to see where this economy is likely to take us in terms of customer service. Actually, we could get 90 percent of the answer straight from an actual headline in the business section of *USA Today:* "BellSouth CEO committed to customer service." CEO Duane Ackerman attempted to explain how his company for the tenth consecutive year came to be rated as first in service among local providers. Asked if service was getting better or worse, Ackerman said, "Expectations are higher." He took away some of the sting when he said, "Good service does not drive up costs. Over time, it reduces costs."

At the top of the following page was a headline that read, "Start-ups turn flat panel TVs into works of art." The story was about Harry Chandler who, on a whim, "put a frame around a monitor hooked to an old PC, hung it on a wall and showed family photographs and art . . . at parties; people just stood there, mesmerized."

And here's my point: What Chandler had done was turn technology into an experience. And today, Chandler has made a business out of providing art for owners of flat panel displays, allowing them to enjoy the technology in an *all new way.*

Starbucks also has joined the game. At the bottom of the page was another head-line: "Starbucks to put digital music on the menu." The gist of the new service was that while you were slurping your morning latte you could preview music, with a whopping 250,000 online tunes from which to choose. While you placed a to-go order for a double mocha skim milk tall, your selections would be burned to a CD for you to take a portion of "that Starbucks feeling" back to your home or office.

> **P** *O S* **P** *o i n t*
>
> You cannot easily separate a product from the service experience. And, the service experience will have an even greater role in the purchase decision, especially when the products under consideration are similar.

Check out the words of Phil Leigh, ana-lyst for the online newsletter *Inside Digital Media,* as he interpreted what this move by Starbucks would mean to the rest of the music industry: "This is what CD retailers will have to do. Bring a social environment to the experience."

It may be more accurate to amend that statement to read, "This is what all retailers will have to do. Turn buying into an experience, a Pos-itively Outrageous Service experience."

TREND ADVANTAGE #I: DECLINING LEISURE

In 1972, I heard a keynote speaker say these exact words: "By the year 2000 the biggest problem in America will be what to do with our spare time. Thanks to the personal computer, Americans will finish their work by midweek, perhaps as early as Wednesday afternoon. And then they will be looking for something to do!"

A show of hands please. How many of you are ahead of this dumb-head trend? I don't see a single raised hand. Why? Because Americans are working more hours per year than they worked a generation ago.

By 2000, three quarters of American families were dual-income families. With two breadwinners at work, most American families are enjoying a high standard of living. In fact, the average American has twice as much buying power today as in 1952. But with two wage earn-ers in a family, we are left with a society that's long on dollars but short on the time in which to spend them.

In 1985, the average workweek had already topped 49 hours, caus-ing available leisure time to decrease by a full one-third in little more than a decade.

Because time is at such a premium for many Americans and, what could be more personally involving than one's time, unexpectedly fast service will be received as Positively Outrageous Service, a gift almost of life itself. After a customer has decided to purchase, we are working on *his or her* time.

Small businesses often have a distinct speed of service advantage over their larger, slower-moving competitor. As Stanley Davis says in *Future Perfect* (Addison-Wesley Publishing, 1987): "Time is a small business strategy and resource."

If speed of service is a major advantage, when it comes to leisure, quality of service will be the competitive edge. With fewer leisure hours to spare, Americans will increasingly be on the lookout for high impact experiences. The businessperson who can bring entertainment value to even such mundane chores as groceries will be king.

The small business person has considerably more creative freedom and control over the operation. But beware! A creative entrepreneurial spirit occupying a position of corporate power can set even large organizations buzzing.

Crazy Ed and Hot French Bread

All I wanted was a box of cereal, a can of fruit cocktail, and a newspaper. She wanted me to have French bread. Not really ordinary French bread but hot, fresh, would-you-like-to-smell-it French bread. She pushed a cart draped with a red-and-white-checkered cloth up the cereal aisle. I thought she was on her way to the deli. Nope. She was hawking, actually hawking French bread in the aisles of the supermarket.

As she docked her cart next to mine and squeezed off a quick smile, the PA system exploded: "Goo-oo-ood afternoon, Albertson's shoppers! Come on down to the deli and pick a pack of Crazy Ed's deli fresh pizza. You can take 'n bake or pick it up hot to go right here in our deli. So come on over and see why Crazy Ed's pizza is the right choice for lunch!"

No waiting, personal service, a great entertainment value. Even grocery shopping can be a Positively Outrageous Service experience!

When leisure time is limited, consumers will be drawn to where the entertainment is the best, even if it's to be found in unexpected places.

TREND ADVANTAGE #2:
QUALITY BECOMES THE RULE

In the old west, the Colt 45 was known as the great equalizer. Big man or small man, a large-slug revolver tended to blur the differences. As we approached the turn of the 21st century, the computer had already helped eliminate many of the differences in product quality. Today, almost every complicated manufactured product is a high-quality product. The choice is no longer between premium quality and imported junk. Today, it's more a matter of differences in color, style, and features.

Not only will quality be the rule, but also quality products will be affordable. Technology, high and low, has resulted in prices on some items actually declining in real dollars. Think about electric drills, TVs, VCRs, even frying chickens! This means that more than ever service will be *the* point of difference.

Dr. William Wilsted of Ernst & Young has studied how various issues of quality impact the buying decision. According to Wilsted, there are three dimensions of quality that drive the purchase decisions:

1. Effective. Does the product perform as advertised?
2. Responsive. Will the product be delivered on time?
3. Personal. How does the customer feel about the purchase?

Wilsted's own descriptions are a bit more academic, but we'll report his numbers exactly. According to Wilsted, while the provider perceives that the personal relationship with the customer weighs in at only 10 percent of the buying decision, the customer gives it a weight of 70 percent!

In an age where the aspects of quality that can be measured by the physical sciences will be ever more standardized, the social interaction of service will acquire increasing significance.

One additional factor of quality straddles the border between product effectiveness and the personal relationship between buyer and seller. That is the dimension of design. A product that works according to design is not necessarily a product that is designed according to the work. Only those companies with the closest relationship with the customer will be able to design products that most accurately target customer needs.

TREND ADVANTAGE #3:
BUYING HABITS ARE POLARIZING

Okay, so service is indeed *the* competitive advantage. But what if I don't want service? After all, there are some products that are more like commodities. Take toilet paper as an example. Most consumers don't particularly need or even want service with their tp. Give it to me soft and give it to me cheap.

As the new century unfolds, the American middle class is growing as the richest and poorest segments are shrinking. Yet, at the same time, our buying habits are tending to the extremes. More and more consumers are discovering that many product purchases don't require service. For those commodity-like products such as gasoline, toilet paper, laundry detergent, and so on, American consumers are flocking to the discounters.

The amazing thing is that the money we Americans save on the necessities is going right into the purchase of luxuries. It is not at all uncommon to see a luxury automobile being fueled at a self-serve filling station. Look in the parking lots of the growing number of whole-sale-to-the-public or so-called warehouse stores. You'll see luxury cars belonging to owners who don't feel at all uncomfortable shopping in a warehouse for commodities, before reporting to the beauty salon for a manicure and facial.

It's important to notice that even the budget-conscious, do-it-your-self types are not settling for subpar products. They expect the quality. It's in distribution that they are willing to compromise. "Okay. I'll pack it myself. I'll buy it in bulk. Just give it to me cheap and make sure it's the good stuff."

For the heads-up entrepreneurs, it's important to realize that dollars saved at the discounters are waiting to fall into the open hands of businesses offering personal-touch boutique-style services.

TREND ADVANTAGE #4: NAISBITT WAS
RIGHT ABOUT HIGH TECH/HIGH TOUCH

Nearly two decades ago, John Naisbitt in *MegaTrends 2000* (Morrow, 2000) identified a trend that he called High Tech/High Touch. It is the tendency to balance the tensions of a hard-edged high-tech world with the soft, calming amenities of high-touch endeavors.

More fast-food meals meant more gourmet meals cooked at home. More commuting through rush hour meant more bicycling on country roads. This is a trend that both continues and plays directly to the outrageous server.

High-techies will be easy picking for businesses that will surprise them with individual service and the opportunity to become personally involved with the selection, production, and serving of their purchases.

Today, more Americans are working from home. According to the National Association of the Self Employed (NASE), four million Americans own microbusinesses, a number that is growing exponentially as technology makes home offices more and more attractive. For the most part, these workers will be high-techies working with their computers and roaming the Internet via wireless and cable. When they do get out, they'll be hungry for more than lunch. They'll want to see a friendly face. They'll want, perhaps expect, a little conversation.

Because Positively Outrageous Service is the most involving, touching kind of service, the trends favor those businesses that serve outrageously.

TREND ADVANTAGE #5:
DESIRE FOR CUSTOMIZATION

In Henry Ford's day, it was "any color you want as long as it's black." Today, thanks to computer-assisted manufacturing, it is becoming increasingly cost-effective to customize. You can still achieve the economies of mass production and custom produce on the same line. To a computer-directed laser cutting device, it doesn't matter or even slow the system to order item number 38,615 a quarter-inch larger.

When things can be custom produced at will, then there will be a rising demand for custom *service* as well. "What do you mean you can build me a car to my personal dimensions, but you can only deliver it between 9 and 5?"

And custom service can even apply to a commodity. "How do you customize a commodity? You standardize the commodity and *customize the services* that surround it," says Stanley Davis in his book, *Future Perfect*.

Watch Out, McDonald's!

"Hello. Nonnie's Café 27!"
"Hi! What do you have for dessert tonight?"

"All we have left is fresh pecan pie."

"Sounds good to me but my wife isn't nuts about pecan pie. What's for tomorrow?"

"What would you like?"

TREND ADVANTAGE #6:
AN AGING CONSUMER

"I didn't realize that we were living in an age where service was the exception until I took my daughter shopping. I couldn't find what I wanted, so I said, 'Let's ask the clerk.' My daughter looked at me with embarrassment and said, 'Oh, Mother!'

"I realized then that there was a whole generation out there that had come to feel they were not entitled to excellent service," says Linda Finlin of San Antonio, Texas. Kids don't have a high expectation of service.

If this were 1965, this book on service wouldn't have been written. Quite simply, books, seminars, and videotapes on service exist only because their moment in history has finally arrived. In the 1960s, you could pretty much open a restaurant, theater, or youth-oriented retail operation and stand back to count your dollars. Don't try it today, unless you know exactly what you are doing.

Those kids that hung out in front of the skating rink or miniature golf course in the '60s are today's largest market, both in terms of numbers and disposable income. Pay attention to those boomers. If you can predict the tastes of the baby boom generation, you can see the retailing future.

If the kids aren't yet interested in service, their parents, on those schizophrenic off-days when they're not filling the Mercedes with bulk tp at the wholesale club, more than compensate, as they demand ever higher levels of personal service. And why not? They have a disease called shopping fatigue.

In 1989, the *Wall Street Journal* surveyed Americans and discovered that three quarters of those surveyed planned to curtail their acquisitiveness, having fulfilled their material needs. It was the beginning of the end of retailing. At the time, Francesca Turchiano, in *American Demographics,* said that "the majority of Americans may now want to clear their closets and shop for new experiences, not new merchandise." And Stanly Buchin, senior vice president, Temple, Buchin, Sloane, said, "The over-45 crowd used to hate spending money and trying new things. Now they're spending their money on experiences rather than assets. What was once a great market for Cadillacs is now becoming a great market for travel."

Did that happen?

Well, yes . . . and not yes.

It seems as if retailers found more stuff we had not yet dragged into the house. Shopping became an Olympic sport. But Americans, at least 52 percent of them, still say they have taken care of their material wants and intend to focus on things they really need. (Thanks to BIGresearch for the numbers previous and immediately following.) Americans, 43 percent of them, are becoming more practical, or at least say so. And 24.4 percent claim to have reordered their life priorities, and maybe they have, since 36.7 percent and 32.4 percent say that in the past 30 days they have deferred dining out or entertainment expenses, respectively.

Whether an aging population is good news or bad news is entirely up to you. It seems clear that if you are selling experience, such as travel and education, you may be in the right place at the right time. But even if your product is Cadillacs, you will still do well if you make buying and owning a Cadillac an experience rather than a simple purchase.

According to Dr. Ken Dychtwald, in his landmark book *The Age Wave* (Bantam, 1990), Americans over 50 represent only 25 percent of the population but control 70 percent of the total net worth of U.S. households, " . . . and account for a whopping 40 percent of total consumer demand." Dychtwald called these people "seasoned consumers."

"Even though they pay attention to price, they are more willing than younger people to pay for quality and service that will make their purchase cost effective in the long run," he writes.

So business is presented with a consumer who has the money to buy but already owns the world. Actually, the world is the only thing the consumer doesn't own, and it will be the travel agents, who in effect "sell the world," who can expect to really clean up. (That sentence is from the original version of POS written in 1990. I did not anticipate the World Wide Web and what it would do to travel agencies. It turns out that I was half-right. Those that specialized in tickets have pretty much disappeared, while those that specialized or were able to adapt and sell service and experience are the only ones left.)

In fact, those monoliths of retailing (regional shopping malls) will quite possibly be among the first visible casualties of an aging, changing consumer base. Think about it. Are shopping malls designed for people in a hurry? Are stores located in the middle of a mile-long enclosed mall conveniently located? Are most malls havens of high touch in a high-tech world? No, no, and no.

In 1990, the monoliths of retailing, regional shopping malls, were predicted to be things of the past as early as 2000. A whopping 20 percent of regional malls were expected to close their doors, because huge indoor malls were hardly conducive to shopping on a limited-time budget. Did the predictions hit or miss the mark? Well, according to the International Conference of Shopping Centers it's rather hard to say. It seems that no one was actually measuring. And no one at the time had anticipated the advent of a new form of mall, the lifestyle center, a hybrid of retail and hospitality that sets all-new standards for the shopping experience.

What we can say for certain is that survivors will be those who pay attention to the expectations of their customers. And just what will those customers expect? Why, an experience, of course! And better that it be outrageous!

Hey, Ed! Over Here!

You may find the kids eating at McDonald's, but the folks with the dollars and the highest frequency of eating out will be at Lambert's Café in Sikeston, Missouri.

"Mother and I were driving to Houston from Chicago. In Sikeston, Missouri, we started having trouble with the car. We were forced to spend the night at the local Holiday Inn, because it was late and the dealer couldn't get a mechanic to look at the car until sometime the next day.

"The wonderful couple who managed the Holiday Inn told us, 'If you're not going to do anything else in Sikeston, you've got to eat lunch at Lambert's.'

"I had seen a sign that said Lambert's Café, Home of the Throwed Roll, and had remarked to Mother, 'What in the heck is a throwed roll?'

"Well, this couple said we'd have to find out on our own, and they even volunteered to drop us off at Lambert's.

"At 11 AM, there was already a line a half-block long. And I thought, Boy! This place is really popular.

"We started talking to other people in line and found out that they were from all over. One lady told us that people came from as far as Chicago just to eat at Lambert's, because it's the greatest place in the whole world. 'If you want a roll, they throw it at you! Then the waitresses follow with buckets of hot molasses and other things to put on your roll to snack on while you're waiting.'

"Well, I asked the waitress how all this got started and she said, 'Why don't you ask Mr. Lambert?'

"So she brought Mr. Lambert to our table, and he was the nicest gentleman you could meet. He asked what we were doing in Sikeston, and when we told him about the car he immediately got up, called the dealer, and made sure our car was next in line.

"Then he ordered coconut cream pie for us. We told him we were full, but he said you're never too full for his coconut cream pie. And besides, it was his treat.

"In fact, he paid our entire bill! When we insisted on paying the check, Mr. Lambert said, 'Anytime I've been in trouble, somebody has helped me. Maybe when you're in Houston, you'll tell somebody about Lambert's Café. That's how I get my business,'" wrote Jane White of Houston, Texas.

And she did.

And you can buy coconut cream pie cheaper at the discount house. (It's frozen.) Coconut cream pie tastes better at Lambert's Café. It's worth the trip.

Random and unexpected, out of proportion to the circumstance, and the customer is invited to play, resulting in compelling, positive word of mouth and lifetime buying decisions.

DISRUPTIVE THINKING—A LOOK INTO THE FUTURE OF CUSTOMER SERVICE

Any process or technology that alters the economic fundamentals of a market or market segment is disruptive thinking.

The original thinker on economic disruption is Clayton Christensen, author of *Innovator's Dilemma* (Harvard Business School Press, 1997), although he spoke in terms of disruptive technology not disruptive thinking. We've tweaked the definition a bit to suit our purposes.

What Christensen observed was that once in a while a new technology comes along and totally disrupts the economics of an industry. What seemed to fascinate him (and me) is that often this technology is not recognized for its potential until the damage, or at least the disruption, has been done.

Christensen observed that because disruptive technology often requires a substantial investment to implement, the old-tech companies insist on trying to wring more out of existing technology and get killed when the market suddenly turns.

I don't think the concept should be limited to technology, unless you are willing to consider a process, a new way of thinking about how work gets done or how technology is employed, as a form of technology. I'd rather use the term *disruptive thinking,* or DT, and define it simply as any process or technology that substantially alters the economics of an industry, especially one that is unforeseen until its impact is inevitable.

Big box discounters finally got to department stores; Southwest Airlines eventually got to the other airlines; disk drive manufacturers lost out to chip makers; and mainframes finally collapsed to PCs. The Internet killed travel agents and music sellers, and it threatens car dealers, call center employees, and even tax preparation specialists whose jobs are headed to India.

In the mid-1980s, DEC was the heavy hitter in minicomputers, but it labeled PCs as "toys that no one will want." And wouldn't you know it? The year after posting its highest earnings ever the company was hit by the PC revolution. Not a single established player in the minicomputer industry made the transition to desktop PC supplier.

And rather than simply looking at disruptive technology, let's set our sights on asking broader questions about *why* a technology is disruptive.

Not All DT Is Negative

Bill Aycock thinks he has a great idea. He wants to put underutilized, smaller-sized aircraft into a nationwide network that serves smaller markets on-demand and at a cost approximating a first-class ticket. He calls this system AirFlite.

If you are an executive without a corporate aircraft and you need to visit clients or operations in small markets with public airports, AirFlite will be a real boon. Your transportation economics will be positively disrupted, as Bill says, "in the nicest way!"

Not All DT Is Positive

When was the last time you paid the exorbitant rates for using a hotel telephone? If you are an hotelier, no doubt you fail to see the widespread use of cell phones as a positive influence on the bottom line.

Hotels have gone from a rape-and-pillage "we gotcha" attitude to Marriott's most recent offer of unlimited Internet access and unlimited long distance calls for $9.95! The $2 access charge for placing a toll-free number is of another day.

In the past decade, wireless minutes have increased by a factor of 36 times, while both the size of the bill and the size of the phone have decreased precipitously. And hotel operators aren't getting much of the pie. As recently as last year, we found a note in our hotel room saying, "In order to serve you better, we are charging a $3 technology surcharge, so that we may install high-speed Internet service in every room." Who needs it? As I write this chapter from my hotel room, I am beaming back copy via wireless connection.

Not All DT Is Recognized for What It Is

The fact that disruptive thinking is rarely seen from a distance gives it its disruptive power. And, it turns out that much of disruptive technology's impact was unimagined and unintended by its creators.

In 1976, when Lamar Muse and Herb Kelleher drew up the plans for Southwest Airlines on a cocktail napkin, who would have guessed they were planting the seeds of an idea that would, eventually, totally disrupt the economics of commercial aviation? Flying a single aircraft type point-to-point is disruptive thinking at its best. Looking at that napkin who would have predicted that United and Delta Airlines would all be considering SWA look-alikes (United Ted, Delta Song) or figured there would be a JetBlue or imagined that analysts would forecast that SWA and JetBlue would be the only airlines to make a profit in 2003?

And just as good ideas can have surprisingly negative consequences, the reverse is just as often the case. I love the new Transportation Safety Administration. The hassles are surprisingly few. And I really like the video kiosks the airlines now use to allow you to get your boarding pass and negotiate a seat change all by yourself without waiting, without help, and without hassle!

And who is our benefactor? Osama bin Laden. Imagine that! Terrorism as a technology. (That reads a whole lot more flippant than intended, but the fact remains that terrorism may be among the most disruptive of thinking. How do you counter people whose highest purpose in life is the death of innocents?)

P O S   P o i n t

Play "What if." What if your product suddenly became obsolete? What if the competition left the market? What if, what if, what if?

When the VCR was introduced in the late '70s, the fear was that we were about to witness the end of the movie industry. But VCRs didn't kill movies; they created fans, and movie attendance has grown 54.4 percent, an all-time high!

On the other hand, there is Napster and other file-sharing dot-coms. After sharing the definition of disruptive thinking with a colleague, he casually mentioned that his 17-year-old daughter had not purchased a music CD in years, that she and her friends ripped and burned direct from the Internet, and that she passes it off as one of those everybody-does-it things. But what parent would tolerate their kids walking out of Wal-Mart with a stolen CD under their sweater?

Coincidentally, while driving through San Antonio and then later in the week through Los Angeles, we happened across the same sign: Wherehouse Music, a national chain, is going out of business.

Think it can't happen to you? It happened to no less a giant than Motorola. What do you do when your $8 billion semiconductor business goes to $5 billion in less than a year? Fortunately, Motorola survived and prospered mainly because it was looking far enough ahead to react in time.

Who would have thought that a 17-year-old looking for nothing more than her favorite music could close a national business?

What well-intentioned bureaucrat or ill-intentioned terrorist or brilliant scientist with no intentions other than discovery could bring your business to an end?

THE FUTURE OF CUSTOMER SERVICE

Two of the bluest eyes on the planet looked up at me from across the dinner table and noticed a slight tremor in my right hand. I am in the early stages of Parkinson's disease, and the chief symptom is what my doctors graciously term "essential tremor." The symptom is really just an aggravation. When it gets really bad or I have to eat peas, I just switch the fork to my left, and so far, unaffected hand. At 54, I am hopeful of a cure, but I'm not counting on it. The blue eyes on the other side of the table think differently.

"Pops?" the precious face with blue eyes and two missing front teeth was commanding my attention.

"Yes, Princess?"

"What's this?" as she bobbed her little fist, a five-year-old's imitation of my tremor.

"Oh, it's just a little tremor that sometimes comes from getting older."

"Well," she decided, "you should get that fixed." And the eyes disappeared as she went on about her meal without a thought that her Pops might have a problem that couldn't just be "fixed."

And that, ladies and germs, is what the future of customer service will look like. We will live in a world where most things will just happen, where problems will be fixed, and where we will shop for customer service just as we might shop for a new pair of shoes. Price, quality, and convenience will rule the entire buying experience and not just a part of it.

And little girls with blue, blue eyes will grow up with a set of expectations that their parents can imagine but not really hope for. The new customer will expect anything and everything. And if we intend to prosper, we will have to develop new and different ways to serve.

Continued disintermediation, omnipresent communication, near-instant delivery, shifted day parts, mass customization, and a democratic marketplace will shift the balance of power and perhaps even dislocate large sectors of the world economy. And it is happening sooner than you think!

Disintermediation

It's a fancy word with a very unfancy meaning: cut out the middleman and buy direct or at least near-direct. The customer has discovered that there is little or no useful service component. There are some products that we don't need or want serviced. Sell it to us fast, good, and above all, cheap. Toilet paper, laundry detergent, and paper towels are good examples, but rapidly being added to the list are personal computers, clothing, and even furniture and automobiles.

The market is saying, "Let us buy direct and pass the savings along to us!" It's an age-old desire to get more for less made possible by technology rather than the ability to haggle.

"How much of the price of buying a new car goes towards paying the sales guy that I don't like anyway? Why can't I buy from the factory and pocket the commission? If I already know what I want, why can't you just send me the computer direct? There's no need to pay the overhead on a giant store where they don't know me anyway."

Omnipresent Communication

Soon there will be no place to hide. We will be wireless everywhere. This can be great for skiers who have lost the trail but pure hell for the boss who just wants a little time to think rather than react. And what is truly amazing is the ability of technology to leapfrog previous technologies.

We built our house and wired it everywhere with category five wiring in order to anticipate changing technology that might put a computer or advanced featured telephone in every room. It's too bad we didn't anticipate wireless! Why tie myself to the office network when I can sit in front of the fireplace or lounge on my office porch and be connected wirelessly?

Third world countries are skipping copper wire telephone systems, ignoring the benefits of fiber optics, and jumping from Stone Age communications to space age technology by going straight to wireless!

But the biggest impact of technology will be the availability of information. The Berlin Wall fell victim to technology. Too many East Germans saw too much Western television and simultaneously came to the conclusion that they wanted a piece of the action.

Communism in China will fall to the Internet. And the only thing keeping North Korea separate from the south is the inability of North Korean radios to receive any station other than the government stations. You can bet your bottom that Kim Jong Il isn't sharing his collection of Western movies with the neighbors.

If you want to change the rest of the world, start talking!

Not too many years ago, parents could control what their children saw and heard. Not too many years ago, there was a hand on the off button, an eye on the mail, and a question on the itinerary. But today there is too much to effectively control.

If you want to change your kids, start talking.

Near-Instant Delivery

FedEx is a verb. Listen to the conversation in any office, and before long you will hear someone say, "Do you want this FedExed?" FedEx used to be a service of last resort, reserved for those instances where we were surprised by a last-minute notice. Well, we must have become the most surprised society on Earth, because in many cases FedEx has replaced the U.S. Postal Service.

I am, at the moment, wearing a shirt and pants from Lands' End. If I am not mistaken, both arrived at our house via FedEx.

Thanks to the Internet, information is now considered a product. Think iPod, think CNN, think help desk. Once the line between hard product and soft product disappears completely, we will want them both—instantly. What happens in your office (and most of us work in offices) when the e-mail goes on the fritz?

Shifted Day Parts

In the restaurant business, there used to be three day parts: breakfast, lunch, and dinner. (I almost forgot the late night bar run on Friday and Saturday!) That was then. Today, there are vestiges of the old day parts, but as more folks work at home on flextime, the day parts are beginning to shift and blur. In our podunk town, Wal-Mart is open 24/7. Even in a town where nothing happens after five o'clock, there is stop-and-go traffic until well after the kids should be in bed.

Customers want what they want when they want it, not when you want them to want it.

Mass Customization

Burger King had the idea; it was just slightly ahead of its time. Have it your way now applies to anything and everything. Order your new car online, and you can follow its manufacture via the Internet. Having trouble finding shoes that fit or jeans that don't pinch? Order online, and for not much of a premium your order will truly be *your* order.

Democratic Marketplace

No longer can retailers dictate fashion, delivery schedules, or price. If you can't deliver, consumers will vote with their feet and switch to your competition with a few deft clicks of the mouse.

If I don't like what you offer or the price at which you offer it, well, sayonara, baby.

WHAT THIS MEANS TO YOU

No matter what industry you are in, you are going to have to change. And no matter what technology makes you special, it will be mass technology that will force you to become even more competitive.

Customers will no longer understand the need to wait. Whether you repair engine valves or heart valves, your customers are going to want it now. Any time will be customer time. On the flip side, young people today have a different idea about what constitutes being on time. Thanks to the cell phone, many young people have come to regard being in touch (via phone) as equivalent to being on time. It will be fine for the customer to be late and your employees to be late—but not you!

Quality products at a low price will no longer be a competitive advantage. Anybody can buy anything from most anywhere. And they can get it even cheaper on eBay—whatever *it* is! Product that is not custom will be a commodity, and soon even custom products will be commodities.

What will be valuable? I believe customers of the future will pay for privacy and for a relationship. In the future, omnipresent communication will put a premium on privacy. When cell phones first appeared, only the elite could afford them. In the early years, owning a cell phone was such a status symbol that you could buy fake cell phones just to impress your friends. In the future, not having to have a cell phone will be a status symbol.

Relationships will be valuable, for a while. Right now, people and products that respond to the unique needs of a consumer are of great value. To do this, marketers will have to become more skillful at learning about individual customers, and customers will have to rethink their ideas about what information they choose to regard as private.

A POSITIVELY OUTRAGEOUS SOLUTION

6

THE HISTORY OF POS

As the former director of training for a major fast-food fried chicken chain, I pretty much was *the* source for expertise on running one of those operations. Well, maybe not *the* source. The truth be told, maybe I didn't really know as much as I thought I did.

I was officially titled the National Director of Training, and then we built stores around the world and I guess it would be fair to say I was the International Director of Training. As a matter of fact, had we built restaurants on Mars or Jupiter, they pretty much would have named me the Intergalactic Director of Training.

But to my way of thinking, I was just your basic God of Training. I had a nice corner office at the Puzzle Palace and could have stayed at the job forever, except for one small detail—the franchisees didn't pay much attention to the God of Training and that was very frustrating.

I would walk into their restaurants overflowing with ideas for improving their operations and putting dollars in their pockets. Did they listen to me? Not even! I was admittedly pretty young to be a God of Training, but still, they should have listened. Instead, they would look at me and think, *If this kid was really all that smart, he wouldn't be working for corporate. If he was really smart, he would own one of these on his own.* And they would offer me lunch and then shoo me out of town.

So the God of Training left the Puzzle Palace and set off to find his fortune in the fried chicken business. He opened his little restaurant in an even smaller town and quickly discovered that there was truth in that old saw, "Those that can, do; those that can't, teach."

Sales started off slowly and then tapered off from there! We were dying, until that lucky day when we discovered Positively Outrageous Service. In a matter of months our sales nearly doubled. We didn't change our menu. We didn't lower our prices. We did change a few employees and the way we went about marketing. There was much less discounting and a whole lot more fun. We started to get serious about having fun and our sales began to climb. Employee turnover dropped to almost nothing. And all it took was a touch of POS.

And now, we are about to do it again. Simultaneous with the commencement of writing this updated version of the original *Positively Outrageous Service*, we are embarking on the buildout of an independent restaurant named Sporty's, a Casual Café. It's in the same small town where we had the franchise restaurant, only this puppy seats nearly 200. We are literally putting our money where our mouth is, and this time we will be putting to work all of the things we've learned since the last time around.

WHAT IS POSITIVELY OUTRAGEOUS SERVICE . . . AND WHAT IS SIMPLY OUTRAGEOUS?

Positively Outrageous Service is the story you can't wait to tell. Everyone has a tale about a favorite restaurant, airline, or retail shop. Some of us have stories about manufacturers and distributors. But all of us have stories that are so good we can't wait our turn. In these stories lie the secrets of retailing success, and in these pages those simple secrets will be told.

That is the good news. In other news, it is true that only a few will serve outrageously. POS is unexpected service delivered at random. Sometimes, the customer is invited to play along. POS is both out of the ordinary and out of proportion for the circumstance. It is a memorable event, and is so unusual that the customer is compelled to tell others. POS creates lifetime customers.

The inner secret of POS is that it establishes a personal relationship between the server and the served.

We know that the shopping-fatigued customers of the 1990s will be looking for "an experience," just as they fervently scouted the malls looking for products in the 1980s. But POS has been around probably for centuries. And it should not be reserved for aging baby boomers. Indeed, every customer in every business or industry should be considered a prime target for POS.

Service, according to Webster, "is something done for others." It's something useful—I'll add desirable—provided in *addition* to goods purchased.

Positively Outrageous Service is something more. Here are some words that go well with Positively Outrageous Service: *surprise, fun, unexpected, not necessary, playful, caring, entertaining,* and *outrageous.* POS is out-of-the-ordinary service delivered in such a way that whenever you get into a discussion about your favorite restaurant, vacation, tailor, grocer, or—yes, friends, it is possible—government agency, this one positively outrageous experience is the one you relate to above all others.

WHY POS?

> *"The rewards from POS are outrageous in themselves. My good moods quadruple, opportunities for POS become easier to spot, and the job becomes more enjoyable. The most exciting thing about being an innkeeper is having the ability to go 'over the top' with Positively Outrageous Service."*
> KAREN BOND, INNKEEPER, RIVER RUN, LADNER, B.C., CANADA
> (FROM THE PROFESSIONAL ASSOCIATION OF INNKEEPERS
> INTERNATIONAL NEWSLETTER, *INNKEEPING*)

Here's a rhetorical question: If you do something for a customer and the customer is unaware that you have done it, did you really do it? This is analogous to the old saw, "If a tree falls in a forest, did it really make a sound?" (One off-take to this is: "If a mime works in a forest, does anyone really care?" Or as Buns likes to tell it: "If a man speaks in a forest and there is no woman present to hear him, is he still wrong?")

The point is simple: If you do something for a customer and the customer is not aware, you have added to the cost of the product (or service) without adding to the value. Smart operators are careful to serve lovingly, while managing to let the customer know the whole of what has been delivered.

Invisible Cleaner

If you think you've had interesting jobs, consider the work of Chris Ballard who was an invisible cleaner: "Years ago, I took a year off following graduation from high school. I spent the best part of it working straight nights as a cleaner at Kodak's Toronto plant. What a hellish job for someone who's a morning person and who thrives on working with people, not in isolation.

"Anyway, I never saw the office workers whose premises I cleaned, and they never saw me. I was the *Invisible Cleaner* who magically removed their grime and trash in the night. If coffee was spilled on the floor, chances are they would leave most of it knowing the cleaner would get it. Most would leave their desks a mess, making it harder for me to dust and tidy. And the washrooms . . . well, enough said.

"About three long months into this routine, discouraged, exhausted, upset with myself for getting into the situation (but needing a good-paying job to afford college), and angry with the people I cleaned for, I decided that either things would change or I would quit.

"The problem, I knew, was that I was the *Invisible Cleaner*—anonymous, invisible. I figured that if they didn't know who I was they wouldn't care about me or what I did.

"So, I invited them to play. At first it was fun stuff, like refilling their office candy jar and leaving a note from the Night Cleaner Fairy. Then, despite the unwritten rule that said cleaners had to vanish before office workers arrived, I began to hang around a little longer to dust and introduce myself.

"At Christmas, I decorated the door of the cleaner's closet. It was in a well-traveled hallway and really got attention with its flashing colored lights, cardboard Santa, and best wishes to all 'my workers.'

"Once while dusting a desk, I found a $20 bill hidden beneath the desk mat. I put it back with a note: 'Thanks for the tip, but $20 is really far too much for tidying your desk. Five dollars would be plenty.' I heard about that one for months.

"People began to notice me, say hi in the hallways, leave funny notes, and thank me for the candy and the extraspecial jobs I did cleaning up after them.

"And another interesting thing began to happen. They began to clean up after themselves. Coffee was mopped up, overflowing wastebaskets emptied, desks tidied, apologetic notes left for big messes, cleaner washrooms . . . a miracle!

"I'd inadvertently discovered what happens when you give POS, invite people to play, and generally humanize the situation."

MORE KUDOS TO POS

"To be honest, Positively Outrageous Service doesn't feel like it should be something extra, but rather something we should be doing automatically. The guests give plenty of clues as to what will make things special for them, and since we're in the business of serving the public, we may as well just follow the clues. While it may take a little extra time, this *is* what we do after all, and it's what gives us pleasure.

"Whether it's fixing macaroni and cheese for three little kids whose parents' car died and they had to miss out on McDonald's, to slipping a split of champagne into a room when you learn the guests got engaged, to taking guests who love antiquing to yard sales before breakfast—it's just part of the fun! We even learned how to roast chestnuts when one guest recalled memories of their first date, a carriage ride in Central Park drinking hot chocolate and eating roasted chestnuts.

"Looking and listening for the clues is all it takes."

Ann Rascati and John Cartwright, Owners and Innkeepers, Liberty Hill Inn, Yarmouth Point, Massachusetts (from the Professional Association of Innkeepers International newsletter, *Innkeeping*)

A CUSTOMER EVALUATION FORM

If you really want to wow the customer, you must invite him or her to play. Positively Outrageous Service is participation service, and the trends favor those who reach out, touch, and involve the customer.

There are zillions of ways to play with your customers if you are willing to be creative. However you choose to be playful, you are giving the customer a good dose of something magical—fun at an unexpected moment.

One day after giving our manager his performance evaluation, he said, "I wish we could evaluate some of our customers!"

"Great idea!"

And we did. (See Customer Evaluation on the next page.) Sure we gave away a few meals, but only to our regular customers who were due for a freebie anyway. And think about the conversation when they got back to the office!

"How was lunch?"

"Great! I got my evaluation and it looks like I need to improve."

"What?"

CUSTOMER EVALUATION FORM

Customer is: Orders:

_____ Regular   _____ Too predictable

_____ Irregular   _____ Eats like a bird

                                _____ Eats lots of bird!

Miscellaneous:

_____ Please wash your car or truck. It's giving us a bad name.

_____ Please wash. *You're* giving us a bad name.

_____ Your bookie keeps calling here by mistake.

_____ Just what is it that you put in your tea?

_____ Is that your real hair?

While you're reading this, we're fixing your order, which is on the house today. It's our way of saying thanks for your business and for being a friend of _____ .

Sincerely,

Scott & Melanie Gross, Owners

_____

Poultry Management Technicians

"My evaluation. I got my customer evaluation, and it said I was doing good but could use a little improvement."

"I don't get it!"

Well, our customers got it. As one of them said, "You can eat chicken anywhere, but you can have a good time only in a few places."

Invite your customers to play, remember their names, support causes they hold dear, be fanatical about your product—do these things and more and your customers will leave saying, "Wow!" And when it comes to being top of mind, you'll be king of the mountain.

7

INVITING THE
CUSTOMER TO PLAY

"Showmanship is the art of giving products personality–yours!"
T. SCOTT GROSS

"That's just what I've got! That's just
what I've got!" shouted the hawker. His face was beaming and his pockets were bulging as he outsold competing vendors at least two to one.

What was his secret? Lower prices? Special product? Not at all. He
simply drew the customer into the game with his cleverly constructed
pitch. "Ice cold beer!" tells you exactly what product is for sale. It's easy
to reject without either looking or thinking. But "That's just what I've
got!" invites the customer to look and then decide.

In sales, looking is half the selling. The art of showmanship whether
practiced at a circus or an elegant restaurant is indeed the art of drawing
attention.

• • • • •

Frank Liberto was the National Association of Concessionaires'
Showman of the Year a few years ago. But in truth, Liberto is a showman every day. Maybe it's a genetic characteristic passed along from his
father. But whatever the source, Frank Liberto has more pizzazz in his
little finger than most of us possess in our entire being.

He seemed an ideal source for a definition of showmanship. Oh,
sure! The dictionary defines *showmanship* as "presenting an idea or
product with pizzazz," a definition that catches the concept all right but

fails to communicate the deeper meaning that true showmen express wherever an audience of 1 or 1,001 is about to be dazzled.

Late one wintry evening, Frank and I wrestled for an hour by phone until we finally had at least the germ of a more fitting definition. We knew intuitively that showmanship is the art of selling the sizzle and not the steak. But it was Frank who insisted that the showman's personality made the difference between simple marketing and true-to-form show- manship.

"It's the personalization of the products you sell," offered Frank. "If you think of your products as part of your family of offerings, it is much easier to personalize the sale."

Too dramatic, I thought, but definitely on the right track. Frank continued that showmanship was not simply selling a bag of popcorn. It was a matter of selling "hot, fresh popcorn" with the added value of the seller's personality tossed in.

We tried again: "When you bring the character and personality of the individual together with the character and personality of the prod- uct, you have showmanship."

That was better but still a bit cumbersome.

Frank said that the personal involvement of the seller was the key we had to focus on. "If products can't qualify as a part of your own per- sonality, you shouldn't sell them. Showmanship only works with prod- ucts you believe in."

Slim sold novelties at San Antonio Mission baseball games. "That's just what I've got!" was his line. No matter what he had, the public turned to look. Then Slim turned his personality on to the product. According to Frank, "Slim wouldn't take out a poor product. It didn't have his name on it, but it had his personality on it."

We decided that personality is the key to defining showmanship. We also decided that a personality with a healthy dose of chutzpah was probably ideal.

We tried again: "Showmanship is the art of giving products you be- lieve in personality—yours." (And it doesn't hurt if your personality is a bit peculiar!)

• • • • •

Showmanship is everywhere, and you don't even have to look because, done right, showmanship reaches out and snatches your atten- tion!

"In the unlikely event of a loss of cabin pressure, oxygen masks will fall from the overhead compartment. Reach up, pull the tube to straighten, and put on your mask as demonstrated. If you are sitting next to a child (or someone who is acting like a child), put your mask on first!" (Southwest Airlines flight out of Dallas)

· · · · ·

It was early on a foggy Sunday morning as a dozen or so weary travelers tossed first their luggage and then themselves into the National Rental Car courtesy bus for the expected boredom of a ride to the terminal at Chicago's O'Hare airport. Wrong!

A tall, lanky young man levitated himself into the driver's seat, adjusted his tie, turned up his smile, grinned into the wide mirror, and, using a PA system designed for monotoned announcements, shook the sleepy inhabitants of the bus back into first person.

"Gooooood morning, campers! Welcome to National Rental Car. And ain't this going to be the best day ever? In fact, it's early but I'm already . . . " And with that, he slam-dunked a cassette tape into a player that promptly spit out the Beach Boys refrain, "I'm picking up good vibrations. I'm getting those excitations."

The doors hissed shut and the bus lurched forward as our driver-deejay launched into a nonstop commentary interrupted only by a medley of greatest hits from the '60s. By now the passengers were awake, laughing, and taking turns trying to outshine an obviously turned-on, tuned-in driver.

Suddenly both the bus and music stopped. "Ladies and gentlemen, we are about to travel the most treacherous part of the parking lot. I don't know if the contractor was out to lunch or if he was an ex-Navy man, but you are about to experience 'the wave'!"

Without another word, only an ear-piercing war cry, our pilot whipped us at full speed over a parking lot that did indeed resemble the sea during a storm. We held tight and laughed all the way to the terminal.

Not one of us wanted to be first off and miss the rest of the best show in town.

HOOK, DEAL, CLOSE

Really good showmanship is often nothing more than jazzed-up salesmanship. There's a hook, the attention grabber that captures, perhaps demands, your attention. The hook is so different, bizarre, or funny that you cannot help but notice.

"That's just what I've got!" is a hook. So is "Ladies and gentlemen, welcome to Houston!" when it's announced by the flight attendant as your plane touches down in San Francisco! A hook is a head turner.

The hook turns into or sometimes is part of the deal. You could use the term *offer,* which is gentler and more sophisticated. But a showman of the old school would be more comfortable with the term *deal.* A deal is one of those "for you and you only, today and today only" propositions. You've heard it at the county fair just before you paid an outrageous price for a vegetable chopper or a knife you can use to either slice tomatoes or cut timber. It's a funny thing about these deals; you know you're being conned, but it feels good so you play along anyway.

The last to come is the close. It's the asking for the sale. That's when the carny at hand figures some clever means to get your head bobbing up and down and your wallet out of your pocket. All showmanship doesn't have to involve money, even though you may easily ask, "Well, why not?"

Michael Hurst, former president of the NRA, had bugs on the menu at his 15th Street Fishery Restaurant in Fort Lauderdale, Florida. That's right—bugs! Hurst is a showman who nearly flipped when he heard about a shrimplike seafood caught off the coast of Africa called bugs. "I had to have it!" he said. And so, it turns out, did many of his customers.

Just the fact of adding a menu dish called bugs becomes a simultaneous hook, deal, and close for adventurous customers. Diners at 15th Street Fishery have come to expect the unexpected. After all, this is the same place where a live cow was displayed for a month in the waiting area as part of an employee-created promotion. It is also where the entire Ohio State marching band paraded through the dining room at midnight one spectacular and very memorable New Year's Eve!

Bugs on his menu, some would say, bats in his belfry. And then there is the problem of all that cash in his registers!

ONE FOR THE MONEY, TWO FOR THE SHOW

We've said it elsewhere: Offering the customer an experience along with the product will be a significant competitive advantage. Why? Because technology and stiff competition have made quality the rule rather than the exception.

Other than innovation, which will provide only the most fleeting of advantages, service will be the last frontier. Fortunately for the small business, the service advantage belongs to those who will think creatively and react quickly.

The good news/bad news of innovative service is that it is easily copied. Still, we've all heard the slogan "often copied, rarely duplicated," which serves as a warning that creating opportunities for showmanship, or "participative service," will not be enough. Managing others to serve lovingly, outrageously will be the trick of the decade.

"One for the money, two for the show, three to get ready, and go, man, go!"

What once was a cute way of starting a kid's game becomes a challenge to those who will serve positively outrageously. Get *one* for your money, the expected. Then get *two* for the show, the unexpected. Showmanship is itself an unexpected added value.

Some have made showmanship an intrinsic, built-in, highly advertised part of the product and that's fine. But, delivered as an unexpected bonus, a little "show" takes on even more value. Remember the first principle of Positively Outrageous Service: it is random and unexpected.

Knowing that you are always going to be well treated adds value and the excitement of anticipation. Not knowing how that good treatment will be manifested adds a sense of mystery.

County Fair, the amusement park mentioned in *Service America!* by Zemke and Albrecht (Dow Jones–Irwin, 1985), routinely self-evaluates its performance in customer terms of friendliness, cleanliness, service, and show. That's not a bad idea for a business that caters to customers actively seeking a good time. But then, what customer wouldn't enjoy being shown a good time in the course of any transaction?

QUALITY, ACCURACY, SPEED, AND SHOW

Any business transaction could be evaluated in terms of quality, accuracy, speed, and show. Give me a quality product, delivered exactly to my liking, do it quick, and you've got a perfect picture of a well-oiled, efficient organization. But involve me in the process and make the purchase an experience and you've got the touch of showmanship that will make you more than outstanding—you'll stand out!

• • • • •

She wears a short, low-cut dress, mesh stockings, and black garters. How do I know? I've seen 'em, and so have the kids who secretly hope to join her performance at the bar. Did I say kids? Performance? Bar? You bet!

She's an old-fashioned saloon hostess at the Old San Francisco Steakhouse in San Antonio, where they know intuitively that a little showmanship is just the right ingredient to improve the flavor of already excellent steaks and seafood.

Each night, young women in the traditional garb of an 1890s beer hall, climb on top of the bar and perch delicately in a velvet-roped swing. A garter-sleeved pianist bangs out honky-tonk tunes as the hostess swings in ever-higher arcs across the bar. The bar itself must be 30 feet long, maybe longer. The crowded dining room grows quickly quiet as both musician and swinger increase their tempo. Finally, toe outstretched, the hostess rings a cow bell suspended from the ceiling at the farthest point in the swing's movement.

Naturally, the crowd goes wild to this scene, which is repeated several times nightly every day of the year. Of course, we know she'll ring the bell, but like the crowds at the car races, even though we don't want anyone to crash, no one wants to miss the thrill of the moment.

At the Old San Francisco Steakhouse, the swinging hostesses further milk the moment by trick swinging, if you could call it that, plus the obligatory test swings granted to the several children who inevitably race to the end of the bar to watch.

Huge blocks of slice-it-yourself Swiss cheese further enhance what is only the merest hint that you're being naughty. After all, the ambience is of an 1890s bawdy house, be it ever so elegant. And, being left totally on your own to whack off as much of the 20-pound block of cheese as you wish isn't much different from having free access to the cookie jar.

Quality food quickly served exactly the way you want it makes the Old San Francisco Steakhouse an excellent restaurant. But face it. Excellent restaurants aren't that uncommon—but a girl in a velvet swing? Well, that's entertainment, and just enough showmanship to keep the parking lot and cash registers full!

YOU BET YOU CAN!

It is possible to teach showmanship. It is even possible to teach showmanship to someone who has little or no natural desire to entertain. It's just not an easy thing to do.

To promote showmanship in any operation you must:

- Hire showmen (show-offs).
- Create opportunities for "show."
- Invite the customers to play.
- Reward showmanship.
- Be a showman.

At the Macaroni Grill restaurant, the very talented staff will visit your table and absolutely knock you over with beautifully performed selections from well-known operas. This is a customer treat that could not happen without a crew that enjoys performing, never mind the talent required. Reluctant performers are not going to sing a cappella in a crowded restaurant.

Tableside opera won't occur without the blessing, make that encouragement, of management. Management has to design the service experience such that "performers" have both time and permission to entertain.

At Macaroni's, customers are not forced to play. You want opera? Ask for it. Unlike some operations that send musicians with their palms up to solicit table to table, Macaroni's is a class act. Customers may request a ringside performance or simply enjoy the moment when nearby guests are serenaded.

Showmanship, unrewarded, will not persist. What is interesting, though, is that for many the opportunity to be at play with the customer is a reward in itself. Being "at play" is more than having fun on the job. It implies a sense of trust and freedom, something too infrequently seen in business situations.

In fact, neither flamboyant showmanship nor gracious, subtle Positively Outrageous Service is likely to occur where freedom and trust have not been thoroughly established.

One additional element usually found only in an "in fun" environment is the costume. Costumes or masks have a way of working magic on both the entertained and the entertainer. Employees who may be reluctant to play with strangers (I guess their moms had something to do with that) will often experience an almost complete personality change when given the opportunity to perform from the safety of a costume.

P O S **P** o i n t

Joking with your customers creates feel good, because the natural assumption is that you won't play with someone you don't like.

Regardless of who you hire or how you structure the job, it is unlikely that you will ever see employees inviting customers to play unless the boss leads the way.

The most fun airline in the sky, Southwest Airlines, got that way only through the leadership of Herb Kelleher. As proof, I offer the example of recruiting ads that feature Kelleher costumed as a rather poor Elvis Presley imitation and tagged with the headline, "Work in a Place Where Elvis Has Been Spotted." (Interested folks who dial the 800 number are greeted with the Southwest rap hotline, a further sign that Southwest is a fun company looking for fun employees.)

On a smaller scale, the assistant at our former restaurant learned a trick that could best be described as a bar stool puzzle, one of those foolers that idle drinkers play on one another. He tried it on our drive-through customers to great results. Wanting more, he approached with the suggestion that we teach any interested employee a simple magic trick.

I just happened to have had with me an easy but mystifying trick called two-card monte. Within minutes, we had several budding magicians trying their new sleight-of-hand skills on delighted customers. In only a few days, their repertoire had grown to four or five tricks, and several of our regulars had jumped into the act with some of their own.

Our manager often started the day and the play by coaxing a smile from a slow-to-awaken customer with his magic. Even though the customers enjoyed the magic trick, it was the humor and genuine childlike approach of the employees that made the moment. The line that always got the biggest laugh was the one our manager delivered after he had dazzled one more surprised customer. "If you liked that," he'd say, turning with a mischievous grin to our team leader, a grandmotherly sprite, "Come back tomorrow. I'm going to saw Frances in half!"

> Employee: "I'm sorry ma'am. There will be a 30-second wait on your fried chicken."
> Customer (at drive-thru): "No problem."
> Employee: "Well, I need to warn you that it's going to be even hotter than usual. In fact, if you bite into it too soon, your lips will fall off."
> Customer: "I'll be careful!"
> Employee: "That's what they all say. But then they look in the box and it looks so good and the smell just jumps right out at them and . . . boom! Before you know it—lips! All over the drive-thru. No problem for us though. We just sweep 'em up and sell 'em for bait!"

UNCLE BERGIE

My grandfather was Uncle Bergie. No kidding! Grandpa was one of America's first deejays spinning his 78s at restaurants and nightclubs throughout northern Ohio and Indiana on behalf of the Berghoff Brewing Company.

Grandpa was one of an army of early showmen who "worked the boards" in the heyday of vaudeville, just before there was television and ad agencies (and before showmanship as an art form was nearly forgotten).

One of the early showmen was Donald Duncan, who in the 1930s elevated person-to-person marketing to a science. Duncan was fascinated by the Chinese invention the yo-yo. But Duncan, who must have been an interesting person, studied the device and made a small but significant design change.

Duncan put a loop in the end of the string that enabled the yo-yo to sleep at the bottom of its trajectory. More important is the fact that this ability made possible any number of tricks. You remember them— loop de loop, walkin' the dog, and, of course, rock-a-bye baby.

Duncan must have been puzzled by that old mystery of physics: "If a tree falls in the forest and no one hears it, does it make a sound?" Duncan wanted to make certain that the entire world heard about his invention.

No doubt there were other inventions and entertainments at the time. And most, probably, were more worthy of attention than a simple yo-yo. Working on the principle that it is indeed better to stand out than even to be outstanding, Duncan created a simple plan to make the Duncan Yo-Yo a household word.

What plan do you have for making your product, service, or name a household word?

Duncan created an entire cadre of showboating, traveling hucksters who became modern-day pied pipers as they spread the word from town to town. They put on demonstrations and held contests; in short, they did any and everything imaginable to create awareness. They beat the drum so loudly that an entire generation of youngsters became hooked on what was no more than a pair of wooden disks and a short length of string. Hardly a kid in America grew up without owning at least one yo-yo. And everybody knew that owning a Duncan meant having the very best.

Today, showmanship is alive and well. We just don't use the term because, thanks to the likes of Duncan and P.T. Barnum, showmanship came to be thought of as gaudy and tacky, definitely a quality of the beer and circus group. So who are today's showmen?

Aircraft services: Showalter Flying Service. If you are a pilot, you know about Showalter's famous customer service. If you are not a pilot, a visit to the Orlando Executive Airport to see how they do it will be worth the effort. Fast, friendly, and done right.

Dine-out desserts: Cold Stone Creamery. These folks make me smile, and you'll smile too when you visit Cold Stone Creamery. We were pleasantly shocked when on our first visit the counterman asked, "Would you like a song with your order?"

"A what?"

"A song. I'll show you!" And with that, three smiling young faces delivered a song and dance routine that blew us away!

Airline: Southwest Airlines. If there is any doubt, just go to the front of this book and reread "The Christmas Man." SWA would have to fly upside down for me to believe they weren't showfolks of the century. Come to think of it, if they flew upside down I'd add another century to their title!

Hardware: Sears. I couldn't believe it either when I saw myself typing S-e-a-r-s, but there is no denying the testosterone-laden Craftsman merchandising displays cause instant tool drool for any real man and quite a few real women!

Automobiles: Mini Cooper. Not being a car guy, I had to go straight to my good friend and car consultant Fred Vang in Santa Fe, New Mexico. I pitched the Audi A8, the new-body-style Corvette, just for its cool factor, in the hope that Fred would be impressed, but he wasn't. When I finished he just said, "Mini Cooper."

"Mini Cooper? Fred, it's not fast and it's so tiny, you expect a troop of clowns to come piling out!"

"That's it," Fred shouted into the phone. "Here's a car that if looked at in the light of day doesn't meet any of the buyer's driving needs, but it has so much personality that it inspires real passion."

And personality is pretty much the heart of ownership.

Casual dining: Hooters. While researching for Sporty's, Buns and I visited more than 20 Hooters and were consistently amazed at the quality of the food and ofttimes near-perfect table service. Yes, the uniforms can be a distraction, and no, the concept isn't for everyone, but any way you slice it the Hooters group has showmanship down to a science.

Lodging: DoubleTree Inns. OK, it's the cookies. Nobody has quite managed to make such a big deal out of something so ordinary. When they reach into that warmer drawer during check-in, it's as if the world was for but a moment Atkins free!

Runner-up in this category belongs to Hampton Inns. I know, they aren't what you would call a luxury hotel, but darn it, they've figured out how to make Doritos seem luxurious.

Clothing retailers: Lands' End. One visit to Dodgeville will be all it takes to convince anyone that Lands' End has done more than anyone to give its service personality, not pizzazz, not flash, just plenty of Midwest wholesome personality. With live online chat and personalized shipping service, Lands' End has done better than any company I know at growing large yet serving small.

Lingerie: Victoria's Secret. It's beginning to seem that you have to be sexy to offer showmanship. Not so; it just looks that way. Wait a few minutes and another VS catalog will plop into your mailbox. You'll see . . . showmanship!

Showmanship: the act of giving a product personality . . . yours!

8

COMPETENCE, CONFIDENCE, COMFORT

Our guess is that no one heads off to work looking for a chance to look stupid. So how come it happens anyway? And do you think they realize it when it does? Here are a few "duh" moments we have recently experienced:

"There are no towels in the restroom."
"Which one?"

"You've dialed a wrong number."
"How do you know?"

"I'm in the office today and I'm either on the phone or away from my desk."

"Lady, you seemed to have picked up my garment bag by mistake."
"Well, somebody took mine."

"Your call is being answered by Audix."
"You have reached the office of . . . [pregnant pause] . . . Bill Smith!"

"If you would like to leave a message for . . . [pregnant pause] . . . Bill Smith! . . . [pregnant pause] . . . you may do so at the tone."

"Thank you for calling the Department of Veterans Affairs. Our office hours are Monday through Friday 9 AM to 5 PM. If you know the extension of the party you wish to speak to, please enter it now. If this is an emergency, please hang up and dial 911."

"I'd like a side order of chicken salad, please."
"Do you want that on a plate?"

"Do you have any bran muffins ready yet?"
"No. We don't bake them until later; otherwise we run out too soon."

Even folks who are potentially Service Naturals will, on occasion, look really, really stupid. The reason? Awareness or lack thereof. One key job of management is to train service people to be aware. Service Naturals have the ability to empathize with the customer rather than be self-absorbed.

If there is one thing that sets apart a great manager from a merely good manager, it is awareness. Good managers have their eyes on operations. Great managers notice everything!

Being aware is not enough. For Positively Outrageous Service to occur, you must be willing to both notice and act on the smallest of perceptions. POS is an affair of the heart.

I CAN'T READ

No employee wants to go to work and look stupid. That's not the nature of human beings. We want to do well, we want to show off. If you have ever watched young children at play, their favorite phrase is usually, "Watch this!"

When we grow up we may stop verbalizing our "watch this," but silent or not, it never really goes away. Employees want to perform.

So why don't they?

Often it is a matter of training. Employees do the work the way they think it should be done, and that's not always correct. Do employees ever deliberately screw up? Well, yes and no. Yes, employees sit on the job and sometimes intentionally sabotage their own work. The question is why?

The answer, I believe, lies in the motivations of your best workers. People enjoy doing things that they are good at. (It's also true that they want to do the things they enjoy.) Conversely, employees hate work they have failed to master.

Which employee is most likely not to show up Monday morning, your best performer or your worst? See? I rest my case. Your poorest performers will accept the slightest sniffle as an excuse for calling in sick, but they are not poor performers because they are ill. They are ill because they are poor performers.

One holiday weekend, I decided to organize a treasure hunt for our grandkids and a small band of assorted cousins. We created clues and a story about pirates and set off around the property learning about directions and compasses, all under the guise of searching for treasure.

The older kids were quick to solve the riddles I had planted at each stop. ("Head north until you find a place where you can see stars even in the daytime." The clue was at the base of the flagpole.) Everyone had solved a clue except The Princess. At five years of age, it was all she could do just to keep up. So we decided to help her discover a clue hidden under a rock down by the gate.

Little legs flying, ponytail swishing, The Princess raced to her discovery. She found the rock, triumphantly pulled out the clue, quickly unfolded it, and then froze. Those blue, blue eyes began to tear, time stumbled for a second, maybe two, as The Princess suddenly realized that she was close but not quite close enough.

"Pops! I can't read!" she wailed.

GOOD WORK

A few years ago, I set out to discover how to manage high-performance teams. The idea was simple: Discover how to motivate and manage a high-performance team, and perhaps there would be ideas that could be used to improve the performance of teams in more ordinary occupations. For example, could the techniques of motivating a team of wildland firefighters be applied to the folks at the local laundry?

It seemed logical that the best way to learn about high-performance teams would be to work on them. So, over a period of two years whenever I could squeeze a few days (or weeks) out of an already full schedule, I flew off in our little airplane and lived an adventure. (Please see *Borrowed Dreams,* Our Time Press, 1999.)

I baked pastries and rolls in a luxury hotel in Dallas, performed CPR in a helicopter over Kansas City, and bent iron in the foundry at John Deere. I chased drug smugglers along the Mexican border and sailed an oil tanker out of Alaska.

Some of the jobs I worked were awful with a capital "A," but in the process I was surprised to learn that no matter how awful the job seemed to me, there was always someone who thought the job was a dream come true.

When I was facedown in the dirt in the middle of the night waiting for drug smugglers to fall into our trap, I was not thinking that Border Patrol Agent was a dream job. But the agent I was with thought he had died and gone to Heaven.

Ramming a couple of hundred pounds of dirty laundry into a hotel washing machine didn't inspire me to make a career change. But the guy who was my supervisor had spent the better part of two decades in that hot, humid, windowless hole and thought he was living on top of the world.

While stuffing dirty laundry, inoculating a herd of muddy pigs, or fighting wildfires under a suffocating blanket of heat and smoke, I happened to discover that there are four elements that when present can turn a job into a passion. They are:

1. An element of *Risk*
2. The freedom of *Choice*
3. A visible *Score*
4. Work that *Matters*

Risk

It's too easy to confuse risk with danger. You can risk plenty of things other than your neck. You can risk your job, your bonus, or even your self-esteem. Look at any job where people are happy, and you will see an element of risk. A cop may risk her life, a restaurant owner may be risking retirement savings, and a salesman may be risking a sale. The happiest workers are those who have something at stake.

Show up for a trade show at McCormick Place in Chicago and see how the union workers treat you. What's *their* problem? They have nothing invested other than their time. There is no palpable risk. Workers who are creative and industrious need not apply. They wouldn't last a week. Instead, they need nonthinkers who will sell their souls in exchange for slavishly following union rules.

> **P** *O S* **P** *o i n t*
>
> The most involved workers are the most invested workers. Find a way to make every worker feel self-employed.

Put in your time and wait patiently for the retirement bell. These folks are some of the most abused workers in America, and the hell of it all is that they are doing it to themselves.

What I love about wildland firefighting is that the outcome is never certain. What turns me on about emergency medicine is that the results are never certain. And the big thrill about being self-employed is that the paycheck can be huge—if it comes!

Choice

Before we leave the union, let me say that the rules designed to protect workers are often the biggest obstacles to work that is good in the sense of fulfilling.

Some years ago, a foodservice workers local in the San Francisco area negotiated a contract with such strict work rules that even workers motivated to serve the customer were often at odds with the rules. A server waiting on three guests at a table was absolutely prohibited from adding a fourth chair if an unexpected guest arrived to join the party. Nope, chair moving was deemed the work of the busperson. Allow just anyone to move a chair, and in short order there would be abused waitstaff and unemployed buspersons as far as the eye can see.

At the Javitts Center in New York, I arrived to discover that some of the seats had been placed behind several of the large concrete support columns that dotted the lower-level meeting room. One chair had been set in three inches and directly behind a column. There was no way to see from this chair, even if you were enough of an acrobat to get to it in the first place.

I did the logical thing: I moved the offending chair to the end of the row and was in the process of moving a second when a union member spotted my heinous activity.

The boss was summoned. A room set diagram was found. "See? That's how the plan shows it!"

P O S   **P** o i n t

The happiest workers are those who have some freedom when it comes to deciding how and when the work will be done.

"Does it strike you as kinda stupid?"

My argument went nowhere; there was no choice to be exercised. Finally, I was offered a compromise. If I insisted that the arrangement be changed, there would be a two-hour wait, a minimum crew would have to be used, and I would be charged, I don't remember this exactly, a minimum of four hours' labor.

Score

The master of keeping score in a work environment is Chuck Coonradt, author of *Scorekeeping for Success* (The Game of Work, Inc., 1998). Chuck likes to point out that people will often work harder at play than when they are being paid to work. Chuck says that there are a few important differences between work and play that smart bosses can take advantage of.

When you are at play, there are a few elements that make play more fun than work. When you play, you are likely to:

- Keep score.
- Have freedom of choice.
- Play with kids you like.
- Have a clearly defined goal.

Looking just a little closer at scorekeeping, at every job I worked for the Borrowed Dreams project, the happiest, most successful performers had found some way to keep score.

On the border, we counted illegal aliens apprehended or pounds of marijuana confiscated. On a farm in Iowa, our interest was in bushels per acre. In the foundry, we carefully watched tons of steel moved through our department. Every now and again as I write this book, I hit 'alt t' followed by the 'w' key to get the latest word count. (My goal is to run out of ideas somewhere around 65,000 words!)

The most effective scorekeeping involves scores that are

- always visible,
- posted immediately after the performance, and
- personally posted by the performer.

Matters

P *O S* **P** *o i n t*

How can you keep score at work?

One surprise I had while working the Borrowed Dreams project was that not once in a dozen work adventures did anyone take me aside and say to me, "This is what we do, this is who we do it for, and this is why it matters." Not once.

If the work I do doesn't matter, then perhaps I don't matter. Nearly everyone wants to be a part of something bigger than themselves. When Southwest Airlines was dukingit out with United over the lucrative intrastate routes in California, Southwest employees often gave up days off and vacation time, paid their own airfare, and flew west to assist the fledgling ops crews learning the SWA system in a highly competitive environment.

The United Way has discovered that donations made through corporate campaigns are significantly greater than when those same individuals donate on their own. Is it coercion? Not even. People not impressed by their own individual efforts like to pile on to help push their corporate numbers into the stratosphere.

One way to communicate that the work at hand makes a difference is to help the work and the worker connect.

After a particularly long shift in the Pastry Department at the DoubleTree, Master Baker Antonio Roma had one last lesson to teach. Tony had run me through the ringer by having me bake well over 100 dozen of those famous DoubleTree chocolate chip cookies. (I'll give you the recipe when you can come up with 22 pounds of chocolate chips so we can get started.) I know he had noticed my tired eyes, but clearly he had saved the most important lesson for last.

"Mr. Scott!"

"Yes, sir?"

"We have one more thing to do."

"Just point at it and I'll clean it."

"No, there is nothing to clean or bake. Just turn your apron to the clean side and come with me please."

I did as instructed, and in less than a minute, found myself in the hotel lobby being directed by Tony to take up a position near a small retail area where some of the goodies we had spent half the night baking were being offered for sale.

"Tony, what are we doing?"

"First, the people will smell the cookies. Then, they will come and buy them."

"Fine, but why am I standing here?"

POS Point

Work that matters is good work. How can you communicate what you do, who you do it for, and why it matters?

"Because then they will look at you and think, *Look, he must be the Cookie Man!*"

I got the lesson immediately, but just in case you did not, take a ride with me on Amtrak a few months later. I was working as a cook whose kitchen was rolling along at 70 mph. We had just sent the last of 52 meals up the dumbwaiter to the diners riding on the top level of the domed dining car. Each meal had been individually cooked to order. There were steaks, roasted chicken, and baked orange roughy served with rice or baked potato, steamed vegetables, garden salad, and a choice of dessert.

We were cleaning the all-stainless kitchen and restocking for the next dinner seating. It was all innocent chatter, until I asked the chef if there was something he didn't like about the job.

"As a matter of fact there is." He removed his tall hat for emphasis and continued by saying, "You know how hard we work down here. And you know how much we care about cooking food that's just right. But you are the exception. My guess is that none of the 52 diners upstairs has any idea how their food got to the table. If they think about it at all, I bet they just figure Marriott did a heck of a job catering."

"Well, Chef, I know just what to do. Turn your apron to the clean side and follow me!"

IT'S RISKY BUSINESS

The manager was armed with a gun—a spray gun, that is—and a roll of paper towels. He attacked the dirty windshield the instant she stopped at the menu board at the drive-thru. He and the unseen owner, who was working the speaker from the inside, carried on playful banter while coaxing an order from the customer who was by now laughing hysterically. At the pickup window, the still-laughing woman said, "I've never had that happen before. When are you going to do the *inside* of the windows?"

"I'm not sure," smiled the owner. "Tomorrow we're doing hairstyling, and Saturday we'll be trying our hand at dentistry!"

And the word spread. And it was fun!

Ken Blanchard calls it "stepping out of the box." Jack Welch is said to believe in "change before you have to." Bill Oncken preached the gospel of "standing out" as being even more important than being outstanding.

Whatever you call it, serving outrageously almost always involves an element
of risk. As it turns out, *risk* is one of the best
words in the dictionary. It has semantic kin-
ship with more than a dozen words that
each packs a punch as powerful as dynamite.

P *O S* **P** *o i n t*

Art happens when the
work and the worker
connect. How can you
connect the worker with
the customer?

Risk leads to *adventure, gamble,* and *luck.*
Risk leads to *audacious* and *daring.* Just look
at the wonderful words and the feelings they represent: "Adventure: an
exciting undertaking." Here's a fabulous relative, *adventurer.* It cuts to
the very heart of capitalism: "A person who tries to become rich by
dubious schemes." Entrepreneurs love it, while bankers cringe at the
thought. But what the heck? If bankers were risk takers, they would be
running their own businesses instead of pontificating about how you
should run yours!

And look at another risk-related word: "Audacious: daring or impudent." Positively outrageous promotions are often both daring and
impudent, as they fly in the face of conventional wisdom.

Risque is a kissing cousin to risk. It means "very close to being improper." *Risk,* though, is word enough to describe the conditions of being positively outrageous in your marketing and service: "Risk: the
chance of running into danger; to expose to possible loss or damage."

Does this all sound too far out, too dangerous? Then go work for
someone else. Stay safe in your office. The entrepreneurs of this world
have created millions of job opportunities. They've made millions and,
because it's the very nature of the beast, they've lost millions. But win,
lose, or draw, the entrepreneurs, the risk takers, always are standing
when the bell signals the start of another round.

Besides, psychologists tell us that the number-one indicator of a
healthy mind is the willingness to take a reasonable risk. Think about
it. The crazies are curled up in a fetal position, while the risk takers are
doubled over from laughter as they play out their hand in a game as big
as life itself.

"The first class mind is an independent mind. It is never totally for
hire. The intellectual does not automatically agree with the boss, and he
would not be of much use if he did." (Hedley Donovan, former editor-
in-chief, Time, Inc.)

The best tales of the outrageous all share a common trait: They are
the stories of risk takers who champion the art of playing out-of-bounds.
They are the stories of the offbeat, those who look at conventional wis-

dom and draw unconventional conclusions. They are the stories of people who are "at play" 24 hours a day.

COMPETENCE, CONFIDENCE, COMFORT

Get this: Competence is followed by confidence is followed by comfort. Get the order wrong, and all you are is cocky.

Denny's put me through college one shift at a time. I loved that job! One night while cooking at Denny's, I left the line in the hands of Randy saying, "Let me know when you start to get busy and I'll drop the prep and jump back in and help." I kept watching over my shoulder as I continued preparing a fresh batch of sirloin tips, and Randy proceeded to get busier and busier.

First I noticed that the tickets began to wrap around the wheel. Then I noticed that not all the orders that went out were properly garnished.

"Are you all right?"

"No problem."

"Well, I notice that all the plates aren't garnished."

"Too busy," was the huffed reply.

I grabbed my spat and stepped to the broiler saying, "When you are too busy to do it right, you're too busy!"

Randy had become confident before he reached competent:

- Competent: You know.
- Confident: You know that you know.
- Comfortable: You know that I know that you know.

Train your team to follow the rules and then, when they are competent and confident, give them room to experiment with the boundaries.

If you are the follower and not the leader, then understand this: There is nothing worse than a nervous boss, and nothing makes a boss more nervous than the thought of turning an idiot loose on both customers and policies.

If you want to get the green light to play with the customers and flirt with the rules, begin by demonstrating your ability to follow the rules and routine exactly. And remember, it takes a very competent boss to feel confident enough to be comfortable with you to declare a POS moment.

If you are the boss, here's . . .

WHY YOU CAN'T LET GO

The gurus all say to do it. You know you should. "But, darn it," you say to yourself, "this is a tough business."

Empowerment is a marginally simple concept when you are dealing in the pristine environment of executives and fine offices, but what about the rest of the world? Let's get real! In our restaurant business, for example, we had to have systems, policies, and a whole lot of luck just to keep the doors open.

How the heck do you empower people who may or may not even show up for work? That's a fair question. You don't.

It's not real to expect convenience store operators or building contractors to fall into line with big-time manufacturing and the corporate brethren who occupy tiny office buildings. But there is much that can be done toward getting people to bring their brains to work.

Problem number one: Letting loose of the reins. Problem number two: Getting someone else to grab them!

Split the empowerment issue in half and a big chunk of the problems falls into the lap of management. Face it. Not everyone in management is willing or even wants to turn in his or her keys to the corporate fire truck. Jingling those keys, wearing the hat, driving at breakneck speed to the most recent two-alarm fire is . . . thrilling.

So, here is reason number one for not letting go: We like being the problem solver who rides to the rescue and saves the day.

Some of us like to think of ourselves as totally indispensable. These folks haven't taken a real vacation in years. They can't. The world would collapse if they were out of pocket for more than 24 hours on a slow day. They wear cell phones as badges of courage, little testosterone meters that hang from the belt.

Of course, these are the same folks who die early. They are also the worst managers in the business. How can they say they are running a business when in fact it is the business that is running them?

Still, we are left to face the ugly fact that it's not easy to attract the most gifted, the most qualified, to an industry known for asking people to work long hours in tough environments for not a lot of compensation. But what if even 20 percent of your folks could and would make intelligent, customer-first decisions of the kind that are not covered in the operations manual? Would that translate into happier customers and less time spent putting out fires? Would that really make you unnecessary? Or would it turn you into a hero able to grow on to other things?

What most supervisors need is an all-new perspective on their value to the company. The most valuable managers build teams capable of self-management.

Reason number two for not letting go: Not every employee is ready to accept empowerment. This can be a matter of training or simple psychological makeup.

Before you criticize your crew for failing to think, ask yourself what tools you have given them to support independent thinking. Employees who are unsure of your intentions, and who do not believe they really do have your permission and encouragement to serve customers with abandon, are not about to get creative.

Worse is the possibility that you are smothering them under a blanket of policies and procedures so thick that even those areas not specifically covered by policy are treated as though a policy exists . . . somewhere.

Ask yourself what evidence your employees might have that you would support them if they stepped out of the box—and failed. Some folks never stray out of the box of conventional thinking and strict adherence to policy, because sticking to "that's our policy" and "that's the way we've always done it" is much safer.

If there is one first step to empowerment, it has to be the hiring of people who will, with training, willingly take risks when it comes to pleasing customers. Oh! You thought *you* were the one taking the risks? Not even!

When an employee is faced with the opportunity to defy corporate policy or even plain old tradition, you can bet that they are thinking less of the consequences for the company and plenty about what may fall down around their shoulders. It is the employee who must be the risk taker in partnership with the boss, who must be the trust giver. This empowerment stuff can be quite a stretch for everyone!

Not everyone will accept empowerment. No matter what kind of environment you create, it's not reasonable to expect that everyone will jump on the bandwagon and put customers over policy. This is the simple yet sticky matter of having some employees who just aren't interested. These folks have to go.

Sorry, but even in a market where it is tough to find qualified employees, you have to face the fact that folks who will not accept responsibility simply cannot be left in charge of anything. They are not qualified for the job you are offering.

For the vast majority of employees who are sitting on the fence considering whether or not you are serious about allowing them to make decisions, know this: They come to you with a history that probably does not support independent thinking. We tend to complain about not being able to find trained people, when in fact no matter who we hire, they *are* trained.

New hires come to us trained to do a jillion things, most of which we would rather they not do. In previous jobs, they may have been trained that it's okay to show up late or call in sick at the last moment. They may have been trained to never ever make a decision, because a mistake could bring down the wrath of the corporate gods. They may have been trained that corporate folks talk about quality and service, but when push comes to shove, it is short-term profits that count the most.

Employees, who in previous lives were clobbered for "wasting" an overdone hot dog or a damaged grocery item, are not about to risk stepping out of the box just because you whipped out a trendy new mission statement that tells them to put people first. No, this empowerment thing is going to take some time. But you can do it. It's worth the effort. Your employees will love you. Your customers will thank you. Your family will get used to having you at home.

FALL INTO THE GAP

Hang in there! We are going for a big POS Point! We often ask audiences to tell us how much more effort their employees can deliver if they were really, really motivated. We want to know how much harder highly motivated employees may work when compared to employees of average motivation.

The exercise usually goes like this: "Raise your hand if you believe your employees can, if they really want to, give you at least 10 percent more effort." (Almost every hand goes up.)

"Keep your hand up if you think they can give you at least 15 percent more effort if they are highly motivated." (Most hands remain in the air.)

A few fall off at 20 percent, a few more at 25, and when we get to 30 percent, we see the largest drop. The hands may shake and waiver, but no matter how you slice it nearly every time a sea of waving hands tells the story: Most bosses think their employees are perfectly capable of delivering about 30 percent more productivity!

What would it mean to your business if you could get 30 percent more out of your existing human resources? (Would you fire 30 percent of the staff? Would you sell 30 percent more product? Or would you simply lower your prices and enjoy increased sales?)

I don't care what your answer is. We have something else on our plate—very few employees are working any way near their capacity. We are leaving 30 percent of something on the table, and smart folks are going to want to know how to make a change.

We have, ladies and germs, a motivation gap that is the difference between the performance you are getting now and the performance you could be getting if employees were truly turned on.

MOTIVATION GAP

The Motivation Gap is located just north of the Cumberland Gap. It is quite large and probably responsible for the lion's share of America's poor showing in terms of productivity. (Gotcha!)

There are two causes for the motivation gap: The obvious cause is that American workers have been presented with insufficient incentive to work closer to their peak performance capability. The less obvious cause of the gap is that American managers have learned to expect miserable performance and are satisfied when they get it.

We were guilty of that very thing when we opened our first restaurant. It was always clean but never as clean as it could have been. The service was good but not what I would call great. By the time our sales had nearly doubled, our place was never shinier or more fun. The service had never been faster or friendlier, and the product never fresher or tastier. On those rare days when sales fell to preexpectation levels, the crew would be both bored and disappointed.

Higher expectations account for the improvement. The performance of the crew became noticeable to the general public. And, surprise, surprise—along with higher standards came lower turnover and record sales volumes.

The big question remains of how to close the motivation gap once you have your expectations in line. Well, hang in there. That's coming up soon.

FEEL GOOD

The third trait to look for when you are building your team is "feel good." We've already discussed the point of hiring smilers, people who will extend a personal relationship to your customers. But how do you know when you have a live one on the line?

It's simple. Spend a few minutes in casual conversation. If you wind up feeling good, and you don't have to quantify this scientifically, chances are you've got a winner on your hands. It shouldn't take you long to decide. In fact, if after more than a minute or two you don't have a strong, positive, intuitive message, call in the next applicant. After all, most service jobs rely heavily on first impressions.

The nicest customer comment card we ever received included this simple statement: "Employees seem pleased to serve the customer's needs." That's it!

BREAKFAST, PLEASE

I caught the phone on the first ring. We had polished off *Larry King Live* and were snoozing our way through *Late Night with Aaron Brown.*

"Pops?"

"Yes, Big Guy."

"Um, could me and Blake ride our bikes to your house in the morning and have breakfast?"

"Sure! But you have to come early."

"Can we have waffles and bacon and eggs?"

"They'll be ready at eight."

Just before eight, I looked out the office window and saw two mop-haired boys coming through the south gate. They were bundled for the cold, and even at a distance, I imagined rosy cheeks and runny noses.

"Incoming!" (That's what we yell whenever grandkids or bigger ones are spotted heading our way.) The waffle iron chirped just as the frosted boys pushed open the mudroom door and squeezed by the dog waiting to greet them. Coats were flung over the chair backs as Big Guy and his cousin Blake took the seats that they knew were theirs.

Two glasses of chocolate milk, "blue straws please," were waiting, and in an instant, the first plate of waffles with bacon and eggs prepared just the way they liked them slid across the counter.

"Thanks, Pops. Thanks, Granny Buns!"

Scott's **L**aw
of **E**xpansion

A business will expand in
direct proportion to the
number of winning
employees who can be
found. Hire all the
winners, get all the
business!

Do you think our grandson likes to visit
with us?

Now tell me why.

It's because people like to be where they
are well treated. We mistakenly think that
treating people well is only a matter of hospitality. Treating people well is a secret of
leadership. It is the antidote to turnover and
the perfect prescription against theft. Treating people—employees—well is how to get
the most out of your staff.

It's so simple, yet so few understand the
power.

THE FIRST STEP
TO POS

MicroBranding

9

THE SECRET TO STANDING OUT

You can spend millions on advertising if you wish, but there are much better and infinitely cheaper ways to stand out in a crowded market. And we aren't just referring to techniques for marketing your business. What works well in the worlds of retailing, health care, manufacturing, even government agencies works even better when applied to your work group, your career, even your personal relationships!

EVERYBODY HAS ONE

Everybody has a brand—and just doesn't know what to do with it. No matter whether your brand is Wal-Mart; Fred Smith, CEO; Juanita Gomez, director of training; neighbor; honey; or Mom—you have a brand.

Now you're going to learn what to do with it.

It's easy to feel overwhelmed by the big players with big brands and even bigger budgets. But each of us can be king of our own domain once we learn to manage our brand.

As a corporate weenie, I hated seeing new executives hired from the outside to do things I would end up teaching them to do. I watched them get big stock options and corner offices, while the real work, and often the real thinking, was being done for them. Was it their fault? No. It was mine. I had the ideas and the talent. I just didn't have the brand.

I remember a new vice president of marketing who wore expensive suits and had an impressive education. His work was marginal at best, and he was a lousy marketer for the company. He nearly killed *our* brand. But funny thing, he certainly was good at building *his* brand—his personal brand, his MicroBrand.

Now I understand the concept, and in a few hours, you will, too!

IT'S UP TO YOU

Individual employees rarely think of themselves as branded. Sign the employment documents, show up for orientation, and wait for the first promotion. This is plain goofy. Normal, but goofy. Helloooo! No one cares about your career until *you* care about your career. If you are going to be content taking life as it comes, then sit back, relax, and don't complain.

Dads, moms, grandparents, lovers, and friends all have brands but often fail to manage them. Dad, I know you are busy, but what have you done to manage your brand with the kids this week—make that this morning? Sweetie, honey, or dear, what have you done with your brand lately? Brought home flowers? Cooked a killer meal? Written "I love you" on the mirror? Trust me. There are others out there with good brands who would love to take your place. Now, move it!

Corporate execs think that managing the brand is something the marketing department does. Give 'em a budget, sweat them through campaign approval, and turn your attention to the really important stuff—like reorganization and right sizing.

Franchisees are the worst. They buy the franchise, put up the sign, attempt to negotiate a lower ad fund rate, and then wait for something to happen. What happens is institutional advertising consisting mostly of discount promotions. There may be direct mail, there could be door hangers, but there won't be much local brand building. Oh, there will also be "bundling," which is a French term for "discount faster."

IF IT WAS EASY. . .

When our son was 20, he called the house one evening and said, "Dad! I've decided to move to Kerrville and open my own stereo and alarm store! I think I can do well, and I could live closer to you and Mom."

What followed was a dump of ideas and emotions. I'm his dad, but to tell you the truth, I rarely understand everything he tells me. When the Kiddo speaks, I just hang on and try to absorb the flood of information that washes away any other conversation.

I don't remember exactly how the rest of the conversation went but it was something like: "Well, I'll be home this weekend. Why don't you come up early Saturday and let's check out possible locations," I said.

"I can't wait till Saturday!" (I thought, *This kid is really on fire!*) "I'm coming up tonight. I gave my notice today! I have to open in two weeks!"

Well, we found a great location, and I stood back and watched a master at work. The kid never asked for or took so much as a dime from Mom and Dad. But he did call pretty regularly those long two weeks. He didn't ask for advice so much as he seemed to need a friendly ear.

"Dad! You won't believe this! I have to have flood insurance! Dad! I can't understand why the fire marshal has to get in on the act! Dad! This is the stupidest thing ever! They want me to . . . "

With each outburst, I would just add to his irritation by saying, "Great news, son! If this was easy, everybody would be doing it. There'd be a stereo and alarm shop on every corner."

On more than one occasion, I would be told that he didn't appreciate my sense of humor, but justice was finally served several months after the store opening. Our son quickly established Rod's Stereo Sounds as the place to get good products and great service for a reasonable price. He was so good with customers that the local newspaper sent a reporter and a photographer to do a story that covered nearly a half page and led with the headline, "Youthful local businessman finds a niche—and fills it."

In the center of the article was a photograph of our son standing in front of what he called his Wall of Sound. But the really cool thing was his quote: "If it was easy to have a business, then everyone would have one."

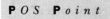

Yes! There is redemption for dads who
stay on message. And there will be rewards
for you when you follow the steps to Micro-
Branding. It's simple, just not easy. Remember, easy may not be all that good.

FOUR KEY IDEAS

A brand is nothing more than an expectation. If the sound of your
name creates an expectation in the mind of a customer, a lover, or your
child, you've got a brand. Which leads us to idea number two: Any message communicated in any way is an act of branding. (More in just a
moment.)

Idea number three? A MicroBrand is any brand intended to dominate a micromarket. And number four, may I have the envelope please?
A micromarket can be as small as a one-on-one relationship.

Idea One

A brand is an expectation. I'd better take a moment to explain.
Many people confuse the brand with the logo. The logo is what you see.
The brand is what you think. The idea is that when you see the logo,
you think the brand.

When you see the Nike swoosh, the logo, you think the Nike brand,
which for our purposes can be summarized as "sports for everyone."
When you see the Lexus badge, the logo, on an automobile, you think
the Lexus brand, which can be summed up as "luxury cars for the lucky
few."

Yes, I know that the brand managers at Nike and Lexus would tell
you that their brands are much more complex than I've made them, but
at least you get the idea.

What about a pin falling in slow motion on your television screen?
You know what that is. It's logo stuff for what brand? Sprint, of course!

And what do you think when you see red and white on a can? For
me, I think *Soup is good food,* one of the huge messages from the Campbell's Soup brand.

Just remember: Logo is what you see and brand is what you think.
See the logo; think the brand.

Now I know I have just crushed one out of two readers who turned
to this chapter thinking they would learn how to develop a killer logo,

one that would smash the competition. Nope. For that you need two things. Second, you need a world-class graphic designer. First, before even that will make sense, you will need a killer brand. So put down the car keys. You won't be needing a trip to Kinko's for a while.

Idea Two

Any message communicated in any way is an act of branding. Good or bad, you are branding all the time.

Roadside delivery. In small towns, nearly everyone wears more than one hat: the plumber may serve on the school board and the county engineer may double as the fire chief of the local volunteer department. My second hat is as a first responder for the county Emergency Medical Service.

It was a just-right spring afternoon, partly cloudy and quiet in our little corner of the world. Buns had decided that we would head to town a dozen or so miles away for an Air Force Band concert. We'd top off the event with dinner following the music and, unbeknownst to us, just a touch of adventure before it all.

I noticed our FedEx driver when he first turned up our hill and deposited a box labeled Lands' End. I figured the package was for Buns and, in a way, it was.

"Isn't it beautiful?" It was more announcement than question. "You've been wanting one of these." Again, another announcement.

But she sounded so certain that I figured maybe I *had* wanted the camel sport coat she was helping me shrug into. (When you've been married for the better part of three decades, there is no sense in talking. You know what the other is about to say, and apparently when it comes to wardrobe, your partner even thinks on your behalf!)

So I polished up the old Ford F150 and at the speed of Fred Sanford headed into town. Had we turned left at the T-intersection, we would have come across this scene: Imagine that you are a 26-year-old female. Your minivan has broken down at the side of the road in the middle of nowhere. In the vehicle with you are your six children, all under the age of 10.

Oh, did I mention that you are in your 36th week of pregnancy, and the baby has decided not to wait another minute longer? If that were you, what would you be praying for? My guess is that the sight of a doctor would be welcome!

But we had turned right instead of left; that is, until my pager went off. I pulled to the side of the road just in case the call was for me and we would need to head back into our service zone.

About that time, a Department of Public Service (the Texas moniker for Highway Patrol) ripped past us in the opposite direction running hot with lights and sirens.

I pulled a U-ey and was rewarded finally by that calm voice of dispatch announcing that Medic 3 and Zone 2 First Responders were needed on Highway 173, where we happened to be.

DPS was first on the scene, and I know my patient must have been somewhat comforted. Then I arrive. From a clean, shiny F150 steps a man who is obviously in his mid-50s with silvery hair to match the pickup and all of his teeth (a huge qualifier in our part of the world!), wearing a beautiful camel-colored jacket.

What do you imagine she was thinking as I removed the jacket, hung it carefully behind the seat, pulled on a pair of exam gloves, and strode confidently toward her van? "This guy must be a doctor! He may even be an obstetrician! Good Lord, at least let him be a veterinarian!"

Do you think I had the heart to tell her I am only an EMT? Should I knowingly step in and ruin the brand I know she had already assigned to the smiling face that had come to make things better? Of course not!

"Good afternoon, ma'am. My name is Scott and I'm here to help. You pitch, I'll catch!"

Ideas Three and Four

Any message intended to dominate a micromarket is a MicroBrand. And idea four, a micromarket can be as small as a one-on-one relationship. I'll explain.

> **P** *O S* **P** *o i n t*
> ___
> Take a trip through your operation with the eyes of the customer and be amazed at the number and quality of branding impressions you are making, often without realizing that you are so doing.

For most business operations—even major retailers—if the world were to end more than a few miles from the front door, they would still depend on CNN to tell them that it happened. Few businesses draw from more than five or ten miles. And for any given location, you shouldn't have more than a passing care about what is happening off this little island of commerce. Dominate the island you are on and let the marketing boys play with their Super Bowl commercials.

It is a waste of resources to spend any marketing money that does not directly target the folks on your island. Should Nike advertise on the Super Bowl? Sure! Because everyone who watches the game is: (1) interested in sports and (2) a potential customer for Nike products.

Should Ed's Corner Drug Shop advertise on the Super Bowl? Of course not! While it may be true that Ed is marketing to his folks living on Ed's market island, Ed would also be spending a pile of dollars on folks who likely will never come close to darkening his door at the Corner Drug Shop. "Thanks for the entertaining commercial, Ed. We'll be watching next year to see what you do for an encore!"

A big part of idea four, the idea that all business exists on a market island, is the fact that the island is likely to be defined by more than mere geography.

Your island could consist of people who consume groceries within an eight-mile radius. It could be folks who purchase exotic hardwoods for custom automobiles. It could even be persons who live in your house and have a wedding band that matches yours.

A micromarket can be very, very small.

MULTIPLE BRANDS

One busy winter workday, I called out to our employees, "It's an all whiz!" That is our signal to hit the restrooms, because we'll be heading to the Burger Basket for lunch. And at the Burger Basket, you don't use the restroom. If you have to go, you just wait; until June would be fine!

So we headed out in two pickup loads, joining a dozen others in the parking lot at the Burger Basket; that is, except for the lone shiny Toyota Camry that stuck out like a sore thumb. See, in our part of the world, everybody drives a pickup or an SUV, some new, some old, but most usually splattered with the buff-colored mud that means spring is about to come to the Texas Hill Country.

I looked at Buns and said, "Tourists."

Inside we joined our neighbors, clad in their Western hats and gimme caps, mixed with the muddy boots, stained vests, bandanas, and oversized belt buckles, and noticed a couple who were sitting and trying to look inconspicuous but failing miserably. They were wearing what we in the speaking business call Docker casual.

I looked at Buns, nodded their appearance, and said, "Tourists."

We sat at the round table north of the counter next to the deuce occupied by the visitors and couldn't help but overhear their conversation, which went like this: "It looks like we're in the center of Podunk!"

If you're wondering if I was offended, I wasn't. Center Point really is Podunk, and we really are at the center of society as far as our society goes.

"I'd bet not one of these Bubbas would know which fork to use at the Hyatt," they continued.

Well, excuuuuse me! Anyone with the sense God gave a goose knows that more than one fork is redundant.

Sitting within spitting distance (and we are all accomplished spitters, thank you) was at least one paramedic; an author; a fellow who flies jets; an aircraft designer; and our neighbor, an international businessman who has flown around the world on the Concorde. Yep, just your average meeting of the Bubbas.

On the way back to the office, I repeated the conversation to Buns, who shot back these wise words: "Well, it looks like they had you branded!"

The moral of the story is simple: We are all *multiply* branded. What are your brands?

I know that when our grandkids ride through our gate at the bottom of the hill, they are not thinking, "Oh, great! We get to visit those folks who wrote all of those books!"

Nope, they're probably thinking, "We're going to see Pops and Granny Buns!" And if we have done our branding well, they are mentally filling in the blanks with "Pops and Granny Buns: Good stories, great food, warm hugs."

Here are two key points about brands: If all of your branding efforts are not congruent, none will have the exact desired effect. And point number two is that no brand is exactly the same in the mind of every targeted consumer.

POS Point

What are your brands and are they congruent with who you are and who you want to be?

Starting with point two, the idea that each of your targeted consumers views your brand at least slightly different is illustrated by the story of Roberta and the 7-Eleven that I used to open the book. (Please take a moment to read that story again, and when you come back, tell me what Roberta looked like.)

I believe I described Roberta like this: "She had dark skin, almond eyes, dark hair, every hair in place. She wore a crisply pressed and starched 7-Eleven uniform with a brass nametag that read 'Roberta.' But the thing I remember most is that she had a smile that made the whole world seem instantly warmer."

> **P** O S **P** o i n t
>
> Great brands live in the imagination and are never exactly the same with every customer.

What did Roberta look like to you? No matter how you answer, I know this for sure: Your Roberta did not look exactly like my Roberta or the Roberta of any other of my readers.

Back to point number one, the idea that for maximum impact all of your brands must be congruent. In the fall of 2003, a commercial appeared that went something like this: Never touch another man's remote. Always wait at least two days before you call her. And never pass up a chance with twins.

Got any idea who belongs to that commercial? When I ask my speaking audiences, someone always guesses that it is a beer commercial, a product for which it would be perfectly congruent but still maybe not appropriate for the kids. Actually, the commercial was for McDonald's, the home of the Happy Meal, and obviously not a good place to either touch another man's remote or pass up a chance to buy two McGriddles for a special price.

THE PROBLEM

If there is a leadership crisis in the business world, it is the inability of top management to accurately define and communicate the brand to both the public and those who are called on to actually execute the brand. Maybe it is fair to say that many brands really are executed, shot before they have a fighting chance!

Now I am going to take liberty with the theory of branding to make an important point: FedEx is a killer example of effective branding. The company can articulate its brand in a minimum of words, so there is no question about what it does. You will remember that FedEx used to be the company to call "when it absolutely, positively has to get there overnight." Nine words so

> **P** O S **P** o i n t
>
> For maximum impact, all of your brands must be congruent with who you are and who you want to be.

defined a company that FedEx became a verb. We have all asked or been asked, "Would you like me to FedEx it?"

Now since the world and markets are not static, the folks at FedEx realized that both their customers and their market area had changed. They were no longer just the folks who hauled documents in the wee hours of the night. People began to want bigger things delivered, and they wanted them to go even further than Peoria. In fact, they wanted them to go so far that it would already be tomorrow at the destination when the package was picked up from the sender. So FedEx pared its description to four simple words promising "the world on time."

Now take a look at Sears, which went to market with a wonderful campaign that invited us to "come to the softer side of Sears." And it worked! I liked it especially, because every time Sears mentioned that it had a softer side, it also reinforced that Sears was still the master of hardware and appliances. The commercials that supported the softer-side campaign were some of the best I've ever seen. You'll remember that some of those commercials compared clothing and jewelry and shoes with items you were likely to find in the tool department. Brilliant!

The next campaign wasn't nearly so much fun. It seemed as if for years the voice-over kept asking, "Sears, where else?" And every time they would ask where else, I would think about . . . where else? And the where else I was reminded of was Wal-Mart. Wal-Mart knows who it is and what it does. And the company can tell you in four words its simple promise: Always low prices, always.

As incapable as management frequently is when it comes to articulating the brand, we are left with the inescapable fact that when it comes to the heavy lifting of branding, the job is often left to the folks in the trenches. And they are the least prepared.

GETTING STARTED: FOUR STEPS TO A POWERFUL MICROBRAND

There are four steps to a powerful MicroBrand. The process is simple; it's just not easy. You must:

1. See it!
2. Name it!
3. Staff it!
4. Market it like there's no tomorrow!

10

SEE IT!

Companies talk about values and mission because it's the thing to do. But having them and living them are two different things.

Corporate cultures are created through a mission statement based on the foundation values. Buy-in from the troops can make all the difference. And it never hurts to have a visible standard of excellence—starting from the top down.

Let's start by breaking this down into bite-size pieces.

All key players must be represented, if not included in the process from the beginning. A key player is anyone who can make or break the process. When creating a values statement, set your guidelines to be limited to a few "core" values, keep them believable, and avoid proselytizing. This is an exercise to define clearly and candidly the values that are currently shaping decision making.

Remember that the corporate values are the combined personal values of each member of the group—like it or not! Be prepared for the brutal truth. Use standard brainstorming techniques that promote getting as many ideas on the board as possible without taking time to argue or be judgmental.

Once you have and can deal with an accurate assessment of current corporate values, it's time to get to the fun part of the process: departing from reality long enough to begin thinking about how things would be in the best of all possible worlds. It's time to begin thinking, perhaps for the first time intentionally, about what values you want to serve as the guiding principles of your company. Remember, this must be a corporate effort that includes all of the stakeholders.

LYNXX

As luck would have it, I had two back-to-back speaking engagements in Orlando. While I love the work, the schedule left me between clients with one giant hole to fill. So I asked for directions, caught the public bus, and rode to the Florida Mall in the hope of finding frozen yogurt and killing the afternoon.

"Sir? What time will the bus come to take me back to the hotel?"

"Easy. Top of the hour, 20 past, and 20 till. Just be out and ready, and the route takes you back the same way you came."

Found the yogurt, walked the mall, and stepped into the wet heat of a Florida summer afternoon about five till the hour.

Top of the hour, no bus. Quarter after, 20 after, half past the hour, still no bus. Twenty till, top of the hour, and now nearly 40 also hot and sweaty people are waiting for the bus. Five after and we saw it and stood in unison, thrilled at the prospect of air-conditioning. The bus arrived but never so much as slowed.

Fortunately, there was a stop sign 20 or so yards from the bus stop. The bus stopped just long enough for me catch up and bang on the door. The door whooshed open with a hiss.

"Excuse me!" My breathing was ragged, my shirt was soaked through. "Excuse me, but didn't you see all those people back there? We're all waiting for the bus. Is this the wrong bus?"

"Sorry, sir. It's the right bus but we're so far behind schedule that our supervisor told us to just run the route until we catch up."

I know you can't believe that, but it's true! It's a perfect example of what can happen when the entire organization is not thoroughly focused on the mission. The driver of the bus and apparently his supervisor thought the mission was to move—the bus. I guess the people were incidental.

P *O S* **P** *o i n t*

The least productive approach to foundation values would be to order up a corporate retreat, negotiate a few rope-and-obstacle courses, and come home with a declaration to force-feed to the troops and hang on a lobby wall.

Once the foundation values are decided, the mission statement can be written to serve as an internal slogan of purpose, a common goal serving as a center of focus. A mission statement should be short, in-your-face, and incorporate your corporate values. It should summarize in less than a dozen words something that in a simple phrase answers this important question: For what purpose does this brand exist?

P O S **P** o i n t

You have different brands that are your life, so why not have different mission statements?

You've seen them. You may even have one. You might even be the person who is guilty of creating one. Give up? Mission statements on wallet cards. Have you ever in your entire life seen an employee reach for his wallet and whip out a mission statement? Me neither! So why waste the card stock?

Mission statements should be in-your-face. Having a mission statement that never makes it beyond the plaque in the reception area is a waste of walnut, brass, and effort. Put your mission statement on a hat, print it on your nametag, or even write it on your sleeve!

We have three mission statements at our house: a personal mission statement (Have fun and make the world a better place); a professional mission statement (Become the number-one brand in customer service management); and a corporate mission statement (Build a business that feels like retirement for us all). And it's perfectly OK to add modifiers to your mission statements.

Our modifiers are:

- Take fun, challenging projects.
- Work with honest, enthusiastic clients.
- Get paid commensurate to our contribution.
- Don't forget to love one another.

If mission answers the question, What is my purpose or the purpose of this team or enterprise? then vision answers the question, What will this person or product be when it grows up? Or better yet is the question, How will I know when the mission has been accomplished?

The vision statement is a picture of purpose fulfilled, describing the desired future in clear terms, providing focus to the mission.

The vision statement is for you. You can include it in your marketing materials. You can paste it into your business plan. In the end, the vision is for you. It's there to keep you on track, to keep you focused on your quest for happiness as you define it.

It stands to reason that if you want to get to happiness, you must first decide what happiness is. Make no mistake, mission and vision are primarily for the purpose of ensuring happiness—yours!

MANAGING OUTRAGEOUSLY

While working as a supervisor at a Louisiana chemical plant, Kevin Coxon was startled to hear his name mentioned on a local radio station. Did he really hear that he had just won the daily "Best Boss" contest? It seemed so unlikely that he was hesitant to call the station to claim his prizes. After all, to win you must be nominated by your employees.

Kevin knew he had been working hard to win the trust of his crew, but best boss? No way. Previous management had had such serious problems dealing with the all-union workforce that the thought of such an award seemed remote, if not impossible.

Kevin's tactic had been simple: honest, open communications at every opportunity. With a little coaxing, he managed to get most of the group to form a softball team, sponsored at Kevin's request by a major contractor to the plant.

At the urging of a coworker, Kevin called the station and indeed he was a winner. But the prizes weren't what excited Kevin. "The best part was that these guys, who were supposedly at odds with management, would do that for me. My boss was shocked. "It's not supposed to be that way," he said.

Now, years later, Kevin smiles and says, "I've still got that plaque."

Beyond assembling a team of winners—employees with the skill and personality to serve—management has only three simple responsibilities:

1. Clearly define the task at hand.
2. Remove obstacles and provide tools.
3. Say thank you for a job well done.

In other words, management supplies the "Go-Power."

GO-POWER!

> G – Goal
> O – Objectives
> P – People
> O – Ownership

W – Work design
E – Example
R – Reward

GOALS

If you don't know where you are going, how will you know when you get there?

Positively Outrageous Service focuses on product and service. Outrageous management does the same. And therein lays the problem. Ask employees to tell you the mission statement of their company, and you are likely to get no more reply than a blank stare. Ask how they personally relate to that mission statement, and you risk inducing a coma.

Once a manager has recruited a new member to the team, the first task at hand is to clearly define the mission. Everything that follows should relate to the mission. Anything that doesn't contribute towards accomplishing the mission is worse than wasted effort. It is actually counterproductive, because time and resources were spent that otherwise could have been put toward the mission.

A mission is forever. Goals are for a year or perhaps as long as five years. Objectives are the small, measurable steps that are milestones on the way to goals.

No company does a better job of defining goals and motivating its employees to reach them than In-N-Out Burgers in Southern California. Here is a company with higher unit volumes than McDonald's and an almost nonexistent marketing program. There isn't a better example of a company that has stayed true to its vision, focused on Four Wall Marketing, than In-N-Out Burgers.

The In-N-Out Burgers concept is perfect for a chain that is national in scope: fresh, high-quality food and fast, friendly service. This could be the motto of a thousand restaurant chains. The difference is that at In-N-Out Burgers, quality is more than a slogan; it's a way of life. In-N-Out Burgers has grown slowly and remained a regional favorite, so that it could keep its eye on the details that make the difference. At In-N-Out, employment starts with a clear vision effectively communicated to even the newest, lobby-sweeping, hamburger-flipping employee.

PURPOSE/MISSION STATEMENT (Prioritized)

In-N-Out Burgers exists for the purpose of:

1. Providing the freshest, highest-quality foods and services for a profit, and a spotless, sparkling environment whereby the customer is our most important asset.
2. Providing a team-oriented atmosphere whereby goal setting and communications exist and providing excellent training and development for all of our associates.
3. Assisting all communities in our marketplace to become stronger, safer, and better places to live.

A Take-Out Order from the Sky

It was an American Airlines flight from Dallas to Maui. The good folks at Continental Bondware had hired me to speak at a gathering of In-N-Out Burgers top-performing managers and their spouses. In-N-Out managers who had met their goals—and that was almost all of them—were being treated and feasted for a solid week at the beautiful Maui Hilton.

When the flight attendant passed by to offer drinks, I jokingly requested a vanilla shake.

"Sorry," she said. "Fresh out of vanilla shakes! But if you look straight down, we're flying over California and the best vanilla shakes anywhere."

"You must be talking about In-N-Out Burgers," said a gentleman seated across the aisle.

"You bet I am, and I could go for one of their burgers about now, too. Why don't I ask the pilot to send you out for lunch!"

There's something about a company that stays focused on product and service. You don't have to be at 33,000 feet to find out what it is.

Power to the People

> *"We take eagles and teach them to fly in formation."*
> WAYNE CALLOWAY, CEO, PEPSICO

Flying in formation . . . that's the goal. But notice just what or who is flying in formation. Eagles, not turkeys.

There's a rather disgusting bumper sticker that reads, "It's hard to soar with eagles when you work with turkeys." What's wrong with this picture? It's an admission that management is not doing its job. On the face of it, you might think it's the employees, the "turkeys," that are being slammed. But think a little deeper. Just who is responsible for hiring? The employees? Of course not! If you don't like the employees, the buck stops at the top!

Turned-on organizations start with turned-on leadership that defines the goals, sets the course, and then goes on a crusade to recruit a battalion of like-minded followers. For every hero of Positively Outrageous Service, there's an unseen hero of empowering leadership.

Donna Paproski of the Mile High Kennel Club has a daughter who works in a hotel. Perhaps the daughter gets her sense of hospitality from Mom, but even a natural tendency isn't likely to blossom without support.

Here's an example: The hotel was totally full when an entire basketball team showed up. The team had traveled all day only to discover that not only was there no room at the inn, there also were no other available rooms nearby. In an act that would make a mother proud, daughter Paproski sent the team to the dining room for dinner, sent the bellman out for rental cots, and converted a conference room into an impromptu but comfortable barracks. All this at no charge.

Outrageous? Of course! And I bet you'd like to steal an employee! Well, I'd like to meet the manager who would empower an employee to serve so outrageously!

POSSESSION IS 9/10THS OF THE LAW

My idea is almost always better . . . because it's mine. Smart managers promote ownership. They know that even a second-rate idea enthusiastically implemented beats a stroke of genius acted out haphazardly. And assuming that employees have second-rate ideas misses the truth by a mile.

The truth is employees have terrific ideas. The problem is getting them to express those ideas. Here are three solutions:

1. Remove the risk from thinking creatively.
2. Reward problem solving.
3. Make ownership the easiest alternative.

Humans learn at an early age to stay within the comfortable confines of conventional thinking. Too often, conventional thinking is no thinking at all.

Raise your hand in school and offer a far-out idea or solution, and all too often the response is anything from rolled eyes to "You've got to be kidding!" Too few teachers and, later in life, managers have the poise and sensitivity to say, "That's an interesting idea! How did you come to think of the problem like that?"

Managers should within reason make well-intentioned failures risk-free. The first mistake should be a freebie. Death by deep-frying is still an acceptable response, but only for a repeat mistake. I'm kidding.

"I notice that you spent $53.48 to have the plastic light cover replaced."

"It cost a little more than I expected."

"I had a similar reaction. Three dollars and 48 cents was about what I had in mind. The $53.48 was a real surprise."

"How did it happen?"

"Well, we couldn't find one at the hardware store that would fit, and since we didn't have the tools to cut one to size and we knew it was a priority with you, we called the electrician to see if he had one."

"Looks like he had a pretty good one!"

"He said he could cut a cover and drop it off on the way to another job. And before I knew it, he had installed it and left a bill . . . and I didn't know what else to do."

"Do you know how to handle it next time?" I said with a tight, very forced smile.

"If it happens again, I'll die before we spend that much money!"

"Exactly what I was thinking."

Reward problem solving, not buck passing. When passing the buck is rewarded over solving the problem, almost inevitably the root problem is that the company has lost sight of its original mission. The Nordstrom employee mentioned earlier had the proper perspective when he said, "We are trained to make the customer, not the sale. We are trained to make customers."

Sales made, forms completed, and phone calls answered are all very effective ways to measure activity. They are lousy ways to measure the level of service. Too often pay plans are constructed in such a way that these deceptive measures of service effectiveness are recorded and rewarded.

If, for example, Marriott only rewarded its telephone operators for answering the most telephone calls per shift, this story would never have been told: Jim Conlan of M&M/Mars arrived later than he wished at the Denver Marriott. Jim described himself as tired and grumpy, a condition quickly remedied by quick, pleasant, "no problem" responses to his requests for a nonsmoking room close to the elevator, a $200 check cashed, and help with his car, luggage, and dinner reservations. Each request, says Jim, was greeted with a smile that said, "I'm happy to take care of you."

"Following a good dinner with good service, I asked the Marriott operator for recommendations for a hotel in Dillon (where there is no Marriott). Within minutes, the operator called back with a list of hotels, complete with phone numbers and addresses."

If Albertson's supermarkets rewarded employees only for cash in the till, you wouldn't have heard this story from Rick Vincent of United Artists Theatres in Denver: "While shopping at Albertson's one evening, I was having difficulty locating an item. Finally, I gave up and took my purchases to the register. The checkout clerk asked me if there was anything else I needed. When I commented that there was something I couldn't find, she left the register and brought it back!"

Problem solving is also rewarded when you defer to employee opinions. "Let me ask Tom to handle that for you. He's our expert in that area." Not only does this give Tom pride of craft, it lets Tom know that he has more-than-expected latitude in his area of expertise.

Here are three suggestions:

1. Provide a range of solutions.
2. Refuse complaints unaccompanied by solutions.
3. Refuse to accept ownership.

When the only tool you have is a hammer, you tend to treat every problem as a nail. Give your employees more tools . . . and teach them how to use them.

My grandmother liked McDonald's sausage and biscuits. She also liked pickles, which was too bad, because try as she would Gran couldn't get Mickey D's to part with a pickle. Pickles aren't supposed to go on sausage biscuits.

So imagine my elderly grandmother walking into McDonald's, ordering a sausage biscuit, and then carefully adding a sin-

P O S   P o i n t

The best way to reward problem solving is to make problem ownership easy or at least easier than problem passing.

gle slice of pickle that she brought from home. Got any idea why "Have it your way" is *not* the slogan of the Golden Arches?

If you forget to pack your own pickle, here's a suggestion. Order a hamburger and ask that they leave off the mustard, ketchup, meat, and bun. Voila! You'll have the pickles you need!

Or you might want to look for someone trained and empowered by Robert Farrell, founder of Farrell's Ice Cream Parlours. Jim Hayes of Careco relays this story: "A new waitress didn't know quite how to respond to a long-term customer who ordered an extra pickle with her sandwich."

"You can order a side of pickles for a quarter," was the response.

"I don't want a side order of pickles. I only want one."

"Well, I can sell you a pickle for a nickel."

With that, the customer picked up her purse and left probably forever. When Farrell received a letter from his unhappy, former patron, he was furious. For the price of a lousy pickle, he was losing a valuable customer.

When Farrell says, "Give 'em a pickle," he means that too often we lose valuable customers over insignificant issues.

Hey, Mickey D's! Give 'em a pickle!

It's probably closer to the truth to say that most McDonald's are owned by quality and service-minded individuals. And you'd have no problem at all getting a pickle, even a handful of them. What is important is that even if it is your policy to "give 'em a pickle," it's of no consequence if your employees aren't aware of their options.

It's fine to have a "give 'em a pickle" policy, but it only counts if you shout it from the rooftops!

Managers keep employee thinking to a minimum when they listen to complaints without demanding that each be accompanied by a solution. Turn chronic, unproductive, spirit-killing complaining into positive action with this simple line: "That's interesting. What are you willing to do to help solve the problem?"

Passing the buck is a skill picked up in childhood. How many *Family Affair* comics have you seen where one of the kids suggests that "Nobody" spilled the milk, broke the glass, or tracked in mud? They say that old habits are hard to break. But this one is an exception if you'll just remember to use these magic words: "Hmmm! That's interesting. How are you going to handle this?"

These magic words are all you need to keep ownership from passing from an employee to you. Bill Oncken, a great teacher and thinker, specialized in the science of Monkey Management.

Bill thought of monkeys as "anything that requires you to make a decision or take action." To Bill's way of thinking, monkeys belong almost exclusively to employees. "It's the manager's job to help employees with their problems," he said at a San Antonio seminar. "And how do you help someone without a problem? Therefore (and here follows a pregnant pause), it's the manager's duty to be the sole source of his employees' problems!"

He meant it!

Employees too often want to give their problems, their monkeys, to the boss. "What should I do?" or "I don't know how to handle this one" are, in the eyes of Oncken, smoke screens through which the aware individual can spot a monkey leaping from an employee's back and landing in a pile on the manager's desk.

"There is nothing as beautiful as the sight of an employee leaving your office with a monkey firmly attached to his back! Because then you can help them!"

The best way to keep those monkeys from becoming airborne is to use these simple words that, like a silver cross wards off vampires, keeps monkeys securely at bay when you say, "Hmmm! That's interesting. How are you going to handle this?"

SEND YOUR EMPLOYEES TO P.E.

Work design—that's an abbreviated way to reference the physical, procedural, and authoritative characteristics of an individual job. The most essential work design element for turned-on, empowered employees is P.E., Project Empowerment. Nothing motivates like results. Unfortunately, too few employees ever see the fruits of their labors. Too few employees are given whole tasks, tasks that have a beginning, middle, and visible, measurable resolution. This is also true of problem solving.

Some years ago, a major insurance company hired a consultant to motivate its vast army of claims processors. The rate of claims processing had fallen frightfully low, a problem the company had attempted to solve by adding more bodies to the sea of desks that already occupied acres of headquarters office space. After careful study, the consultant made a simple, no-cost recommendation: Deliver mail in the morning; pick up mail at shift end.

The recommendation makes more sense when you think about the rest of the job design. Each desk had a large in-basket and an equally large out-basket. Claims came in, were processed, and then dropped into the out-basket. Every hour or so, a mailroom clerk would pick up processed claims and deposit another load of fresh claims.

Since most of the claims processors were women, the old adage "A man works from sun to sun, a woman's work is never done" seemed doubly appropriate. It exactly described the problem: the processors were totally demoralized because they never seemed to be making any progress.

Just about the time an in-basket reached empty, a mail clerk would come by and fill it again. That was bad. Worse, though, was the fact that the out-basket was emptied at the same time. In other words, the employees never had a chance to see the results of their labor.

By limiting mail pickup to the end of the shift, the workers could enjoy a sense of accomplishment.

Feedback delayed is feedback denied. Equally as important as having something that can be physically measured as a sign of achievement is the idea that employees should be able to measure for themselves.

Ken Blanchard uses the analogy of bowling with a sheet covering the pins. You roll the ball, it runs straight and true, slips under the sheet, and a tremendous clatter is heard. Then your boss peeks under the sheet and says, "You got two."

"Two? Hold up that sheet and we'll both count!"

There is the story of Frito-Lay putting counters on their bagging machines, so that the operators could have a visual record of their performance. I'm told that simply adding the counters and requiring the operators to make entries in a production log dramatically increased productivity.

These examples of the relationship of feedback to physical productivity also illustrate the importance of feedback to the more emotional issues surrounding problem solving for customers.

Deny me the opportunity/responsibility of seeing a problem handled all the way to resolution, and you may as well not ask me to help at all. Even if I help a little, it will still be difficult to muster personal, emotional energy. After all, it really isn't my problem.

P O S   P o i n t

Every job should have something that employees can count or otherwise measure as a symbol of tasks completed.

Look at the difference between the valet and the manager in this next tale. Which one had the responsibility and authority to handle the entire problem? And who got the "feel good" of setting things right?

Dan Gallery, of Carts of Colorado, arrived at the Hyatt Chicago O'Hare after a long day, made even longer by a delayed flight and heavy traffic. The valet did not have a pen and asked to borrow one from Dan. Dan's new Cross pen had special meaning, because it was a gift from his wife to celebrate his company's election to the *Inc.* 500.

Later when Dan reached for his pen, he discovered that it was missing, most likely still with the valet. He called the concierge, who, rather than handling the problem, suggested that he inquire at the valet desk. She said she doubted that the valet had lost his pen. The pen remained missing.

A furious Dan Gallery fired off a hot letter to the hotel's general manager. When Dan returned to the office, there on his desk was a letter of apology, a new Cross pen, an offer of three free nights accommodations plus a fruit basket, wine, and complimentary room service!

Of course, we have to give that Hyatt general manager great credit for his customer-saving, out-of-proportion response. Losing a pen is unexpected. Losing a special pen can be highly involving. It took an extraordinary service response to both salvage and increase customer affinity.

But you have to wonder how the story would be changed if either the valet or the concierge had been to P.E. If they had Project Empowerment, the responsibility and authority to handle a problem in its entirety, how much better could Dan's story have been?

It may not be realistic to give valets the authority to order up Cross pens, complimentary lodging, and free room service. Or is it? How would the story play out if instead of a hotel Dan had lost his pen at Nordstrom?

HAND-TO-CHIN

Hand-to-Chin is an entry in my seminar notes. It's a cue for me to act crazy and involve my audience in a quick game of semi–Simon Says. At the end of the game, I'm usually standing on a chair or table facing a sea of laughing faces when I yell, "Grab your chin! Grab your chin!"

Of course, I grab my cheek. And so does nearly everyone else. Not my cheek . . . theirs!

Why? Because when it's all said and done, when theory runs into reality, people learn by doing. Not by listening. Not by reading. People learn by doing.

Monkey see, monkey do. The behaviors that people are most likely to try are those behaviors they see in their environment and can imitate. If you don't see it, you are not likely to try it. If you don't try it, you won't learn it.

And so, for all our fancy training programs, sophisticated lesson plans, handbooks, and flipcharts, in the end our everyday operations are our most effective training program, like it or not.

Whenever you interact with your environment, you have a learning experience, whether or not you are aware of it. Each interaction is followed by a consequence that may seem important but could just as easily be missed as insignificant.

Paul Mudloff of the United Artists Theatre Circuit recalls a childhood experience: "I attended a theatre when I was a young boy at a summer matinee. It was the first time I attended the theatre, and the place was packed. We all waited for the show to start, and when it was time, the theatre manager (owner) walked down to the front of the theatre with his staff and introduced his staff to 600 screaming kids.

"After the introductions, he invited 600 kids to sing *God Bless America* with him, after which he promised we could all scream as loud as we wanted . . . until the movie started. It not only provided a good feeling and a good time, but it also made me want to work for this man as well as attend movie events at his theatre."

Did you notice Paul's career choice? You never know when the example you set will have a lasting, significant impression.

We hired a young man against our better judgment and put him to work in our restaurant. This was years before our volume grew to the point where we could somewhat hide a less-productive employee. At lower volumes, everyone has direct customer contact.

Still, I was confident that in spite of his awkward language and social skills, we could teach him to give at least passable customer service. In our place, everyone could hear both sides of the conversation at the drive-thru. This was because the customer's voice was broadcast via speaker.

The drive-thru became an ideal place to serve as an example, since everyone would hear your service patter as well as the customer's response. When I was at the store, I always went straight for that position, so that I'd have a chance to reinforce the customer service example.

"Playful" was a good description of my approach to service at the drive-thru. Interacting via a metal speaker can seem downright impersonal, unless the server takes extra care to sound friendly and approachable. After a few mornings listening to my example, our awkward, new employee volunteered to take a shot at the drive-thru, clearly the most demanding position in the store.

I reminded him that suggestion selling is important to good customer service. I told him to relax, have fun, and be sure to always offer a drink perhaps by saying, "How about an ice cold soda to wash that down?" How was I to know that his very first order would be to a thirsty construction worker who only wanted something cold to drink?

> **P** O S **P** o i n t
>
> If you are in any way unsatisfied with your employee's customer service behavior, there is only one first step to take. Look in the mirror!

Employee: "Good morning! May I serve you?"

Customer: "Give me a large cola."

Employee: "Would you like some hot, battered french fries to wash that down?" (Huh?)

The customer was so surprised that he ordered the fries, and our beaming employee was so encouraged that he managed to sell a two-piece chicken dinner "to round that out."

Excellent customer service only occurs when employees have an excellent, visible standard that they can imitate and against which they can compare their own behavior. The good news is that the standard is always visible. The bad news is that the visible standard is not always a visible standard of excellence.

As the owner, CEO, or manager, you bear the special responsibility of being the most visible standard.

CARRIES A CHAINSAW BUT GETS GOOD RESULTS

The behavior you get is the behavior you reward. In times of high unemployment, you can get away with "chainsaw" management. But the instant people decide they can find a better job elsewhere, they start to bail out in droves.

An old-time manager just smiled when I proposed an incentive program to help stem the tide of massive turnover.

"Incentive?" he said. "We give 'em an incentive every day: Do your job and you get to keep it."

An interesting concept but worthless.

A manager is the keeper of the rewards. He or she can reward behavior with a smile, a verbal or written acknowledgment, sometimes a prize, or monetary reward. Management looks like this:

Step 1: Hire capable members to the team.
Step 2: Define the mission.
Step 3: Arrange for the tools and time necessary to achieve the mission.
Step 4: Use rewards to focus behavior on the mission.

We're on step four. Step four is the most difficult. Some managers rarely think to reward mission-focused behavior. They remember to punish undesirable behavior while completely ignoring the importance of rewarding good performance.

The problem with this approach is that criticism and other forms of punishment (negative rewards) only serve to *stop* undesirable behavior. They do absolutely nothing to *start* desirable behavior.

Praise and other positive forms of rewarding behavior move the organization closer to the mission. Negative rewards may halt backsliding, but they do nothing to cause a move forward.

Managers who hide the carrot and carry a big stick kill any chance of creative customer handling. After all, who wants to chance getting clobbered if something doesn't work perfectly or fit policy exactly? That's not to say that when things go wrong, managers should ignore poor performance. Even when you do criticize, you should not strip away an employee's dignity.

One of the nicest stories took place at the end of the day at Durrin's Dry Cleaners in Kerrville, Texas. Owner Chet Whatley called his crew to the back of the store one evening right after closing. "I'm sorry for all the yelling I've done around here lately. And I'm sorry for all the yelling I have left to do. But I do appreciate all the good things that maybe I forgot to mention." With that, he presented each employee with a single red rose.

Thank you, after all these years, remains a powerful motivator—especially when delivered sincerely and publicly. But there should also be some tangible rewards for those who serve with pizzazz.

Don't think saying thank you has that much value? Well, take this!

A survey by Dr. Roger Flax, president of Motivational Systems, asked this question: If another company with a reputation for giving recognition and praise offered you a similar job with the same salary and benefits, would you quit your current job?

Now, quitting a job is a pretty stressful act. So making a change just for better recognition is a major decision. Still, more than a fourth (27 percent) of all the workers surveyed said they would leave. Nearly two out of three (67 percent) of those who said they would quit their jobs work for companies where recognition is rarely or never given.

A *USA Today* survey discovered that 44 percent of those currently employed expected to hold the same job for the next three years. Fifty-six percent did not.

Recognition, reward, is a powerful tool. If you are not good at it, get good at it. Your employees are watching. And so are your competitors!

NAME IT!

If there's one critical thing to know about position, it is to grab it first. Whoever grabs it first owns it forever. I'll explain with an example: Say that you own an independent building supply center in a small town. Based on feedback from the contractors who do business with you, you think free delivery would be a competitive advantage. So you offer free delivery and invest in a campaign to let the market know. You even adopt a slogan: "We really deliver—and it's free!"

In a matter of months, the world as you know it grants you the position of free delivery. And since positioning is always against someone or something, you improve on the slogan by saying, "The store that delivers—free!" This implies that the other stores don't deliver.

When your competition notices your success, the best they can do is, "We deliver, too!" Not good. Your competition will have to come up with a different niche, unless you make a mistake or never grabbed it in the first place.

That leads us to a second scenario: You offer free delivery but don't aggressively capture the position. You deliver but don't tell the market. Now your competitor sees your success and goes for the position with the slogan, "Number one in free delivery." Now who owns delivery?

The first to grab a position owns it.

POSITION VERSUS POSITIONING

A position statement is the description of how you want your brand to be positioned in the mind of the customer.

Let me caution you not to make the gap between your position statement and your position too great or your customers won't make the leap. If you discover that where you are is too far from where you think you'd like to go, go somewhere else! Be the best in your tightly defined micromarket; strive for that and the customer is likely to follow, if not actually help!

A position is always compared to or against other brands. It might read as simply as:

> Positively Outrageous Service will become the number-one brand of customer service management. It will be recognized as the name to call when meeting planners want a humorous yet information-packed presentation at conferences of all kinds. POS will be first in the minds of managers and corporate trainers when thinking about their service training needs. It will be regarded more highly than service.

Whatever you do, stand for one thing and one thing only that will help you stand out in the market. Focus. In this one instance it is best to narrow your position. And make certain the one thing that makes you stand out is also a competitive advantage.

A couple of years ago, McDonald's launched what was called the "55 Campaign" to promote the Big Mac. The idea was to celebrate the 30th anniversary of the double-decker, cholesterol-delivery system, and McDonald's did it by discounting the Big Mac to $.55, the same price as originally introduced.

P OS **P** o i n t #1

The position statement describes the position you want to own.

I believe that in most places a Big Mac will set you back in the neighborhood of two bucks, so this promotional price represented a discount of almost 75 percent. You would think that customers would have knocked down the doors for such a huge discount. They didn't. They stayed away in droves.

Why? I think it was that, at such a deep discount, the promotion did not seem believable, and suddenly the flagship of the Mickey D menu no longer seemed either desirable or exclusive.

P O S **P** o i n t # 2

Positioning describes the mental real estate you actually hold.

Robert Cialdini calls it the Law of Scarcity. When there are few of an item, the value goes up. This is even true for items that no one would or should want.

Take the Edsel. In 1959, it would have been "take the Edsel, please." Because in 1959, there were too many Edsels; it was one of the biggest flops ever made by the Ford Motor Company. Not many were made, and not many were bought. The Edsel was just a dog, a marketing idea gone down the tubes.

Today, if you had an Edsel in good condition, it would be worth in the neighborhood of $5,000, considerably more than it was brand new.

And what if we had started with something really cool like a '57 T-Bird with automatic transmission, power steering, power seats, and power brakes? You'd be looking at $41,000.

The opportunity for MicroBranders is this: We have to turn our small size or numbers into an advantage.

One way is to use price as a measure of scarcity. In the mind of the consumer, high price usually equals good:

- "I took her to a high-priced restaurant."
- "She's the most expensive attorney in her field."
- "We bought the best one we could afford."

I have often told folks that if I cut my speaking fees by 80 percent, I would starve to death—not necessarily from lack of money but from lack of sales. At 20 percent of my fees, no one would hire me. Why? Because at those prices, they would reason I must not be good.

Think about a client who wants to bring 250 of its top salespeople to the Hyatt Regency Maui for a sales meeting. The client decides to hire an outside speaker, and because this is also a reward for good performance, sessions are only scheduled in the morning. The rest of the day will be time off for play.

Start totaling what it costs to put those 250 bodies in front of the speaker for a couple of hours. There is salary, airfare, meals, and shuttle, and the Hyatt isn't what you would call cheap. Soon you're talking some

P O S **P** o i n t

Advantage is always defined by the customer.

serious buckos. You could easily be toting up a number in the neighborhood of several hundred thousands of dollars.

Is the company going to hire a $500 speaker? Is a $50,000 speaker necessarily better than a $500 speaker? Well, you can definitely say that one is a better marketer, but you really can't tell from the fee which the audience will love the most.

What you can imagine is this conversation after the speaker bombs . . . "Where in hell did you get that guy? He was awful!" "The bureau said he was highly recommended. He's one of their highest-paid speakers."

And that settles it. Expensive is at least supposed to equal good. And it definitely equals exclusive.

Your job is to do a little price comparing. Find out where your product fits in terms of range of prices. You don't want to be the cheapest, because it's for sure you won't be perceived as the best. If you aren't the best, then think about selling your product or yourself at the low end. Why? Because there is only one place worse than the bottom, and that's the deadly middle. In the middle, you get beat up on price and are looked down on in terms of quality.

If you decide to compete on price, forget any idea of exclusivity and focus instead on believability and convenience. Bill yourself as "the low-cost alternative" and console yourself with the bottom feeders of the market. They won't be the best customers, but you can have them all to yourself.

TAG, YOU'RE IT!

There's hardly anything more important to your MicroBranding efforts than settling on a good—no, make that great—tag line. A tag line is your position statement brought to life.

In six or seven words, you want to tell what you do, who you do it for, and if there are words to burn, why you are the best choice. It's hard to imagine that so few words can work so hard, but they can.

There are no wasted words in a great tag line. Every word works and works hard. There are two tricks to creating a tag line in few words. One is to leave out words that the reader or listener is likely to fill in without thinking. And another is to use words that can be interpreted more than one way.

Look at this favorite from Home Hardware in Canada, "Help is close to home." In one well-built phrase there are several messages:

- Home Hardware is the place to go for help; they are experts.
- Home Hardware is like being at home.
- Help will be given freely if you go to Home Hardware.

Notice how this one plays along so well with the company name, "Visa: Everywhere you want to be." A visa is your permission to travel to exotic locations, and now this Visa is telling you it will be there no matter where you go. Visa could be talking about geography in the literal sense, but it could just as easily be talking metaphorically. Wherever you go in your career or life, Visa will be there for you.

You may have to look closely to see the implied suggestion that the other guys, American Express, MasterCard, and Discover, won't be there.

In five killer words, we got the whole enchilada—the who, what, when, and where of Visa. We even got to lean against the competition without so much as mentioning their names.

Tag lines should, like great brands, serve as mental shortcuts that tell you what the product does, who it does it for, and why it's the best choice. Keep them to as few words as possible; use the right words and the reader or viewer will happily fill in the message, often more message than you ever imagined.

Sometimes you don't even need words.

We like to work with Angel Flight, an organization that connects owners of private and corporate aircraft with patients in need of long distance transportation. We fly all sorts of folks. Our most recent passengers were an eight-year-old boy, who was recovering from major soft palate surgery, and his mom.

At the FBO (fixed base operator), we fueled the aircraft and greeted our customers, trying as best as our limited Spanish would allow to introduce ourselves and make them feel comfortable. As we walked to the plane, a pilot who had been watching this minidrama unfold caught Buns's eye. He applauded silently, hands barely touching but heart fully engaged, as he bid us safe journey and good spirits.

More thought needs fewer words.

A great tag line mentions the unique selling proposition (USP). In a few words, it lets the customer know precisely why this brand is the brand of choice.

Remember to think like a customer. The position statement tells what *you* want the market to think, but it's not necessarily a reflection of reality, the real position that you won. You can try to shape the market with your tag line, but why not let the market do the shaping, especially if it is already heading in your direction?

KitchenAid did just that when it created a new campaign for its countertop appliance division. Research showed that consumers weren't interested in simply having another appliance. Their interest was the food. The appliance was only a means to an end. It sort of puts things in a different perspective, doesn't it?

One KitchenAid print ad featured lemon soufflé pancakes—food! Smaller images of the appliances used to prepare the dish seemed to be almost incidental—exactly how consumers think! A Web site was also listed inviting the reader to click for the recipe. Did it work? The company reported double-digit growth in the first six months.

THE BIG ONE!

Most BIG (Brand Identity Genius) ideas aren't revolutionary; they're evolutionary, a step further along an already beaten path. Tom Monahans didn't invent pizza delivery. He invented "30 minutes or free" pizza delivery.

Herb Kelleher didn't invent air travel, but he added the innovation of point-to-point service at a time when the trend was taking the others to hub-and-spoke terminals.

To create your BIG idea, you might want to start with a little idea or maybe just an old idea. There really aren't as many new ideas as there are variations on a theme. Engineers call this process parallel analysis.

The idea is to find dissimilar industries with problems that are similar to yours, see how they solved the problem or at least how they view the problem, and see if you can adapt or adopt a new idea (to you) for your situation.

Here are several interesting ideas to start the thinking:

Avoid the "Michael Jackson" change. Change for the sake of change can have drastically unintended consequences. Any one change may, by itself, make perfectly good sense. But a whole series of changes considered and made individually might combine for a totally unintended and possibly unwanted result!

Add complexity to make things simple. I'm not fond of the KISS (keep it simple, stupid) principle. It seems all wrong to me. Here's why. It's possible to make things simpler by first increasing complexity. I say, KICK (keep it complicated, kid!)

There is more efficiency than can be measured with a stopwatch. Efficiency should take into account all of the costs in addition to the expense of time. Have you considered the expense of morale? Sometimes we fail to account for the toll exacted when intelligent human beings instead of being challenged to think are denied the opportunity to think and are saddled with boring, repetitive tasks that numb the brain and stifle the chance of future creative thinking.

Incompetence foils innovation. That's another interesting lesson I learned. When people aren't confident in their training and skills, they are more likely to act negatively under stressful conditions. And since innovation is born under the banner of intelligent risk, it only stands to reason that if you include intelligent risk in your organization, you will create a training ground for confident employees who in turn will reward you with innovative ideas.

Give customers an experience. Why? Because they want one. If you are looking for a BIG idea but don't think you are ready to invent a new source of energy or an exotic new technology, then look for new ways to present a familiar product. Customers today want more than stuff; they want an experience.

We met an interesting fellow in northern Wisconsin who had spent nearly two years renovating a huge old Victorian mansion with the intention of operating it as a bed-and-breakfast.

"Is it historic?"

"No. Just old."

"Does it have a ghost?"

"No. It's just a big, old, and now beautiful house."

"Get a ghost."

Get a ghost, get a story. Entertain. Deliver an experience!

THE SHOWALTER BRAND

A deep low-pressure system is working its way across the upper tier states. Last night it dropped visibility to near nothing in a wide band across Wisconsin. Tonight it's holding me hostage at O'Hare International Airport. My 7:09 flight was bumped first to 7:55, then 8:30. Now it's 9:00 and Lord only knows when the bird will finally lift off.

I wish I were flying myself. I would have been home by now.

If you can't be home, then on the ramp at Showalter Flying Service in Orlando will make a good second choice. Showalter is what pilots call an FBO: fixed base operator—in English, a gas station for airplanes.

P *O S* **P** *o i n t*

MicroBrands are built on standing out, and standing out begs for innovative thinking.

If you want the primo example of Positively Outrageous Service, then look no further than the Showalters. Bob and Kim with daughter Jenny and son Sandy run a first-class family business. We may have coined the term, but the Showalter folks own the concept. They were delivering POS long before we began defining it.

And here is a big POS Point: Many people deliver POS because it comes to them naturally, with or without a name for it. Others deliver POS because the boss does it and thereby encourages it. The rest are lucky to get to work in a clean shirt. No matter how cleverly you name it, some folks just aren't going to make the effort to get to WOW! (They're stuck on Woe!)

First the fun stuff.

It had been a long day of flying that took us to Marco Island for a presentation at the Hyatt. We did our thing, loaded our little plane, and hopped over to Orlando for the night and another engagement. Naturally, our target was the Showalter ramp.

Now, you have to get up pretty early to sneak up on the Showalters. (They're so nice we hate to call ahead. We don't want to put them to any trouble.) The Showalters keep a close eye on the Internet, tracking the progress of any flight headed to KORL, Orlando Executive Airport. Every plane has a registration number printed on its tail and the Showalters have a database of all of their customers. Put two and two together and you're busted! The Showalters literally have your number and will be waiting for you the instant your wheels spin on the runway.

This particular night they were, no surprise, waiting.

It was a starry night still new and sporting the heat of a summer day. The blue lights along the taxiway led the way and seemed to promise iced tea, warm shower, cool bedsheets, and a cozy hangar for one of the other girls in my life, N95MK.

The ramp agent raced out to greet us, waving his bright orange marshalling lights and driving the "Follow Me" cart. Instead of leading us directly to a parking space in front of the trailer filling in for their new building under construction, he led us along the curving perimeter of the ramp and then suddenly hooked a right and stopped short. I doused the taxi lights and was a bit taken aback when a forest of orange marshaling wands switched on, revealing a small band of Showalters and employees.

When we stepped from the plane, the sharp beam of a flashlight showed that we had been parked in a field of brightly colored stars that had been painted on the ramp just for us!

And then there was singing. Sung to a fun circuslike tune, it went like this:

> Welcome to Orlando
> We sure are glad you're here.
> We'd like to sing a song for you
> To fill your heart with cheer.
> We think of you quite often
> You taught us how to play
> And now we practice all the time
> Get better every day.
>
> Although we're full of history
> The building is not old
> The trailer cannot represent
> The tons of fuel we've sold.
> The trailer cannot bring us down.
> We'll tell you one more thing,
> We'll never be too serious,
> Thanks to the Chicken King. (Bow)
>
> Soooooooooooo . . . . (swing arms)
> One last time we'd like to say
> We're really glad you came.
> To Scott and Buns, come have some fun
> And join us in our games!

And that's just one great story.

There was the time Orlando was a three-day pit stop at the end of a long week of flying that had left me exhausted and the Little Girl splattered with bugs and dirt from a dozen takeoffs and landings.

"Sorry about the trashy looking airplane. She'll get a bath when we get home," I apologized to the ramp agent who was used to pumping Jet A into sleek and shiny business jets.

"No problem, Mr. Gross. We'll find a place to hide it until you get back."

So, what did we find when we returned? Okay, this one is too easy. They washed the plane, but you probably figured that. Would you have guessed that it was waxed? And how about the huge red bow and ten yards of ribbon that turned an airplane into a delightful package?

That's Showalter. That's POS!

P O S **P** o i n t

First get good, then get great, and then and only then will you be ready for Positively Outrageous Service.

Wherever there are airplanes, you're going to find the orange marshaling wands that are used to guide you to parking and bright yellow wheel chocks that help hold your plane in place once it is parked. No big deal. Well, actually, at Showalter it is a big deal, because they make it one.

On a recent visit we taxied to the ramp and began to look for the agent. This time he (actually it was *they*) was especially easy to spot. Some quick-witted somebody had taken two eight-foot lengths of four-inch PVC pipe, spray-painted them Day-Glo orange, and created the world's largest marshaling wands!

The ramp agent explained with a smile and a wink saying, "Some of our pilots are maturing."

And what would huge marshaling wands be without a set of chocks nearly as big as my airplane! What a treat these folks are!

Walking into the Showalter Flying Service building is like walking into a cool breeze. In the winter months, a Showalter friend appears towing a huge and wonderful Wurlitzer organ. This fellow used to repair organs, the big ones, and when he moves south for the winter he works for the Showalters and brings along the organ. Why not? Gentle organ music turns an already comfortable lobby into a haven from the whine of jet engines just a few feet beyond the door.

Need a little lovin'? Call for Mary Jane, the Showalters retired drug dog, who is normally headquartered in a back office but occasionally trots out to get her ears scratched (or to sit impatiently next to a piece of luggage!).

At Showalter you can get fuel and hugs, rental cars, and an organ concert. This is truly a place where great service and Positively Outrageous Service live side by side.

And that leads us to another . . .

12

STAFF IT!

This chapter couldn't have come at a better time—for me! We are just hiring our crew for Sporty's, a Casual Café. Buns and I are thrilled with our three team leaders and really impressed with the team they are assembling. We have believed from the beginning that success or failure will be determined not by the razzle-dazzle of the concept or the inspiration of the team owners (us). We know that the ability to assemble a team of winners is the most important ingredient. Good leaders need great followers.

Robert Teerlink, former head of Harley-Davidson, has been quoted as saying, "If you empower idiots you get dumb decisions faster." The man has a point!

Staffing your organization is a matter of three considerations. First, you have to run your organization in a way that makes it attractive to the kind of folks you want to hire. I once had a businessman tell me that he couldn't bring himself to respect anyone who was willing to accept a job working for him. (I decided to be accommodating and told him that I agreed!)

Ann Rhoades of People Ink, and one of the original five executive team of JetBlue Airways, is fond of saying that the best hire is the great employee you already have. No, that's not "Zen and the Art of Aircraft Maintenance." What she means is that if you don't lose employees, you won't have to always be looking for replacements. Ann says, "You've got to rerecruit them every day!"

Our take on it is this: Employees don't leave jobs that they love, and they love jobs where they are loved!

At this writing, Sporty's is about 18 days from opening night, and we have nearly hired the entire crew. They are all bright, smiling, poised lovers of people who are itching to work in a fun environment, exactly the kind of folks that people say you can't find anymore. There's not a tongue stud or visible tattoo among the lot.

A few of our soon-to-be competitors have noticed. A couple has even asked our secret. Our general manager is too polite to say it, but I know what he's thinking: "There are great people out there—they just don't want to work for you!"

I'm a bit more sensitive. If good people work somewhere, the only question that remains is why they don't work for you. Fix that and you will have your team.

So the first step in assembling a great team is to not lose the good employees you already have.

Step two is to get clear on what a winning player on your team looks like. The number-one reason for bad service is miscast employees. Simply stated, we seem to insist on asking people to do things they just cannot bring themselves to do. At Sporty's, would you expect everyone to be outgoing? Well, they're not and that's OK. We'll take the introspective ones and teach them back-of-the-house skills. (Hey, even one of the team owners is not exactly the life of the party! I'm the quiet type!)

There is a right job for everyone and someone for every job. The responsibility of management is not to fill holes on a schedule. It is to fill holes with the right personalities, and that begins by at least giving some thought as to what are the right personalities.

Step three is to treat recruiting as the marketing problem that it is. Remember, good people work somewhere so give them a reason to work for you!

For a thorough look at how to put together a winning team, check out my book *Why Service Stinks . . . and Exactly What to Do about It!* (Dearborn Trade, 2003).

FINDING SERVICE NATURALS

Ed McGowan of Bryan, Texas, headed for his parked car. Being somewhat of a neatness fanatic, rather than ignore a piece of trash, he stooped to pick it up and drop it in a nearby dumpster. Ed was surprised to discover that his trash turned out to be treasure.

Falling from what at first appeared to be a discarded envelope was a $100 bill. Attached to the currency was a bill from the electric utility. Also enclosed was a note obviously written by an elderly woman telling how much change she expected.

McGowan, like a retail Will Rogers, has never met a customer he didn't like. He even loves the customers he has yet to meet. Unable to contact the owner of the missing $100, Ed paid the bill to prevent a cut-off of service and took both change and receipt to the police department.

Security experts tell us that 5 percent of the population is pathologically criminal. Some 85 percent of the population is basically good, provided they are not faced with a situation that makes misbehaving risk-free. The remaining 10 percent are the saints of the world. They rarely have second thoughts about following the golden rule. They are the original do-unto-others.

These same percentages seem to hold true for high tolerance for customer contact. Ten percent can't get enough of their customers. Five percent want to be left alone. The vast majority, when it comes to customers, can take 'em or leave 'em.

Joy Wright, founder and president of Personnel/Performance Systems, Inc., says, " . . . as a rule, people who are honest like people and they like themselves." In years of preemployment screening, Joy has discovered that "if somebody is sociable, in most cases, they are also higher in character strength and integrity."

Hiring lovers of customers means finding that one person in ten. Here is where the going gets sticky. First, the likelihood that the boss is a natural lover of customers is also only one in ten. Second, customer lovers aren't job hoppers. They probably already work for someone else. And third, with such a shortage of true customer lovers, recruiting and hiring these winners is not enough to be successful. We must discover how to manage that great "situational majority" in such a way that they too will love on the customer.

Ed McGowan, mentioned in the opening paragraphs, is one of the 10 percenters. Not only is he scrupulously honest, he's also a great lover of customers. You should not be surprised.

Of course, there are exceptions to most rules. Still, seeking the 10 percenters will pay off. Not only will they love on your customers, it is also more likely that your money will make it to the bank.

In a little while, we'll give you several dynamite interviewing tips to help you make your final selection. But first you need to know where all those wonderful 10 percenters are hiding.

Birds of a Feather

You heard it first from your mother. When you started hanging out with the notorious Zooberg twins, she shook her finger right under your nose and warned, "Birds of a feather flock together." Hang out with the neighborhood "terrorists" and before long you, too, will be solidly on the road to hell.

The principle, luckily, works just as well in reverse. Find one knock-down, drag-out winner and you're hot on the trail of a whole flock of them! Start with your own employees. Which one is a 10 percenter? Next ask her or him to help you recruit a friend. Don't worry. They won't drag in a warm body. Winners like to work with other winners, and that's exactly what a winner will recommend.

Ask the kid with the "born to raise hell" tattoo to help with recruiting only if you are hiring mercenaries. We have never had an employee who ran with a crowd of neat, polite friends quit without notice or attempt to steal cash or merchandise. It just doesn't happen.

RECOGNIZING SERVICE NATURALS

Positively Outrageous Service is playful. It invites the customer to become involved. Involvement on the part of the server requires a high tolerance for customer contact.

Ron Zemke and Karl Albrecht in *Service America!* report that high tolerance for customer contact is essential if the employee is to avoid psychological overload. In simpler terms, it takes an iron constitution to cheerfully handle large numbers of customers, especially when they arrive in rapid-fire order.

Any business will have its share of superstars as well as a number of just-get-bys. What may not be obvious is that traits that seem to guarantee success in one business may invite failure in another. The same is true for the characteristics required for performing in various levels of the corporate hierarchy.

In the mid-1980s, we ran a psychological profile on several hundred unit managers and assistant managers. The theory was that if we could discover psychological similarities between successful managers, then by hiring new manager candidates who matched the profile, we should experience a lower washout rate during the training process. Also, these psychologically selected candidates should be expected to achieve mastery earlier and turn over at a lower rate.

That was the theory.

In reality, our profile indicated that, indeed, successful unit managers did exhibit personal traits that were markedly different from those branded as unsuccessful. We determined success or the lack of it by a relatively uncomplicated formula involving sales, unit level profits, and sales increases over the previous year.

So far, we had a program that must have come straight from heaven . . . until we looked at the profiles for assistant managers. Much to our surprise, we found that assistant managers in successful stores had decidedly different personality traits than their managers. Too bad. The career path to management included posting as assistant manager!

In short, we found that many of our most successful unit managers had met with considerably less success as an assistant manager. We discovered that our most successful unit managers had management styles that almost guaranteed failure at the next level up, multiunit supervision.

According to our survey, assistant managers worked harder and longer than successful unit managers. That was also true for unsuccessful unit managers, who we discovered actually worked longer hours than their successful counterparts. The best managers, it seemed, delegated only sparingly, a trait that would be certain death for multiunit supervisors.

Conclusions: (1) You can't define a winner until you first define the job; (2) a winner is not a winner in every situation; and (3) your "best" employee may not always be your most successful.

In our operation, we had an assistant manager who was prolific at churning out ideas for serving and promoting outrageously. Unfortunately, he didn't particularly enjoy being the focal point of public attention. Our manager, on the other hand, also contributed to the brainstorming sessions. His ideas were often unusable in their first-offered form, but more than any of us, he enjoyed basking in the limelight.

Fortunately, all the 10 percenters do not look and act alike. Loving on customers does not require every employee to plaster on a smile and walk around in polyester leisure suits with white belts and shoes. Positively Outrageous Service *can* be borderline bizarre, but elegantly engaging service may also qualify as Positively Outrageous Service. To recognize a 10 percenter, though, does not require a degree in rocket science. You need only one working eye and a few minutes of undivided attention.

The following is from the first edition of *Positively Outrageous Service* and is as true today as it was then. In an article on customer service in the *Wall Street Journal,* Dennis Schmidt, assistant vice president of Methods, Training and Security for Delta Airlines, was quoted as saying that Delta looks for high customer contact tolerance in newly hired flight attendants. I asked him how Delta, clearly a customer service leader, manages to select the 10 percenters. Is it testing? Special assessment centers? What?

According to Schmidt, who I promised to report as six-foot-six and good-looking, "there's nothing magic about it."

Oh, yeah? Well, putting together one of America's finest airlines is magic. It turns out that Delta uses everyday garden-variety magic to do it. Delta employs flight attendants to screen applicants because, according to Schmidt, "they've been there" and know at least intuitively what it takes to handle tired travelers and squirming babies.

"It's just a sense or a feeling," says Schmidt. "We try to see if they can carry on a dialogue. They have to be able to exchange information . . . to serve the traveling public."

And there lies the first step to hiring a 10 percenter.

In a world of first impressions, why not let your first impression be the guide? Do you want to be absolutely certain? Then follow this patter exactly:

Scott's No-Fail 10 Percent Finder

It's not unusual to get really angry at a customer. Everyone does at one time or another. Still, there's a big difference between doing something overt like getting physical with a customer and something like gently putting a rude customer in his place. How many times in the last six months have you felt it was necessary to get tough with a customer? Tell me about the worst incident.

If you want to be certain you are not being conned by someone who pours on the charm just to get past the interview, the above line of questioning will do the job. Here's how it works. First you establish a psychological environment that invites the applicant to be normal when you say, "It's not unusual to get really angry with a customer. Everyone does at one time or another."

Next you send a signal that you are aware that there are extremes of behavior and imply you sympathize, though you never say it. "There's a big difference between doing something overt like getting physical with a customer and something like gently putting a rude customer in his place."

In the third step, you ask for an example of getting tough with a customer. Because you have stated that such behavior is not unusual, that everyone does it, and that you recognize extenuating circumstances, the applicant will feel compelled to at least tell you something.

This is psychologically equivalent to "Do you still beat your wife?" Any admission is an admission of poor customer relations. It will be up to you to decide if, under the circumstances and according to your sense of ethics and customer service standards, the behavior was or was not acceptable.

"How many times in the last six months have you felt it was necessary to get tough with a customer? Tell me about the worst incident." In this last step, the answer you get will first tell you how often the individual goes into psychological overload. The second question is the most important. The answer that follows will tell you precisely how this person deals with customers.

The 10 percenter, who because of the construct of your question will feel obligated to tell you something, will tell you that in their opinion getting tough with customers just isn't OK.

Of course, there will be the occasional situation where the customer was physically threatening and even the nicest of the nice will resort to self-defense. But, based on how the incident is described, you can evaluate whether the response was appropriate according to your standards.

That 85 percent majority, though, will more than likely give you an occasion or two where "the customer is always right" went right out the window. Here you must listen closely to the situation and make a determination about this person's service potential.

The bottom 5 percent will quickly weed themselves out. You don't need any coaxing about how to evaluate. "I told the *!?!* to get out and stay out."

Watch applicants who use terms like "stupid" or "rude" when talking about either customers or fellow employees. These terms tell you that even their best service, while it may be word perfect, will come across as forced.

The point to remember is this: You cannot evaluate information you do not have. Unless you ask an applicant questions that reveal customer service attitudes, you won't discover the truth until too late. Remember, too, that after you've asked for a description of worst-case customer service incidents, you must ask plenty of follow-up questions. Mentally fill in the blanks, and the only one who is being interviewed is you.

There really isn't any magic to picking the 10 percenters. Like cream, they will rise to the top. In an imperfect world, it may not always be possible to only hire the very best. But a few minutes spent in casual conversation is all it takes to determine if you are dealing with one of the vast majority who, with proper leadership, can learn to truly love customers.

Singing Pigs

Never try to teach a pig to sing . . . it wastes your time and it irritates the pig. A pig farmer in Lampasas, Texas, taught me a different version: Never wrestle with a pig . . . you get dirty and the pig loves it!

However you say it, not everyone is psychologically capable of extending "feel good" to perfect strangers. No matter how much training, incentive, or innovative job designs you offer, you are absolutely wasting your time on those whose psyche won't allow them to get lovey with a customer. Not only are you wasting time, money, and effort, you also are probably irritating the heck out of them!

Some people have difficulty being warm and friendly with their spouse. And no, I am not calling them pigs. That's just an example. You could just as easily cite the saying, "You can't change a leopard's spots."

We walked into a theater, my client and I, and were greeted by a dour-looking doorman at the ticket drop.

"Your theater is to the right," he moaned.

"So what's with Mr. Excitement?"

"Oh," said the client, "That's Harry. He's a little different, but after a while he grows on you."

"Mold will grow on you. But I don't think I would hire it to greet my customers."

The American economy is increasingly a service economy. Ninety-two percent of all U.S. employees will work in a service industry and account for 85 percent of the gross national product.

Here's a pop quiz: True or false? IBM is a manufacturing company. If your answer is true, try again. As early as 1990, IBM had nearly 400,000 employees worldwide. Only 6 percent (20,000) were involved in manufacturing.

The trend towards a service economy means that every day we are becoming a nation of first impressions. Our daily lives are a series of pop quizzes, instant decisions about whether or not we like a product or service. There's an old saying that "you never get a second chance to make a good first impression!"

The point is simply this: The successful business will neither recruit nor hire employees who do not make a dynamite first impression as they go about the business of making customers feel good.

Hire to the Bench

Stop for just a moment and mentally inventory your crew. Are they all 10 percenters? If the answer, as it most likely will be, is no, then you need to hire. A full schedule means only that you have covered your shifts; it does not mean you are finished hiring. Your tactic should be to hire to the bench. Assemble a team and then continue to hire until you have a team of all-stars.

Too often, we only hire when there is a vacancy. This results in panic hiring. We body-snatch to fill the position. Once filled and the panic subsides, we tend to forget that even though we have a full roster the team is not up to full strength. Management must continually be on the lookout for potential winners. When you find one, hire. The worst thing that can happen is that you will have to expand the business to give your winners room to grow.

The problem with winners is that, like cops, they never seem to be around when you need one. If you are serious about hiring winners, you must be prepared to hire one anytime you find one. When you are served by a winner, pass her a card. Introduce yourself and let her know that you like her style. Better yet, if you have a card or coupon for a free sample from your business, leave one. If she likes you and is interested in your product or service, she will be in. If she isn't happy with her current job, she now knows exactly where to apply.

At the end of especially busy days, we often send someone to a competing restaurant for a change-of-pace snack. This is a little treat for the crew and another way of saying thank you for your hard work. One night it went like this:

"I'd like six chocolate and two vanilla shakes, please."

"Yes, sir!" She was smiling as she noticed the name of a competing restaurant embroidered on my shirt. "Why are you buying milkshakes?"

"Well, we just set a new store record, everyone is tired, and we sometimes like to take a short break before we start cleanup."

"Your change is $1.87." Then she leaned close to whisper, "Do you have any job openings?"

You can't steal happy employees. Unhappy winners are easy picking.

Fit

Almost three of four hires are decided largely over the issue of fit. In the best of all possible worlds, almost all hiring decisions would be based on fit. In that case, you would hire with the idea that you already had such a wonderful crew you'd be careful not to "hire down."

Because businesses are not essentially different from professional sports teams, it makes good sense that every new hire should be evaluated in terms of the potential to hurt or help the performance of the team. If all business were conducted in a large domed stadium with a national television audience watching, hiring would be much different.

The Monday morning quarterback who analyzes and criticizes every trade by the local professional sports team would get religion when it came to hiring to fill a vacancy on the sales team. Instead, because the element of competition is not so obvious in the business world, we end up body-snatching and passing off a poor hire as not all that consequential.

"How important really is the guy who helps load trucks at night?" The real team players of industry will tell you, he's very darned important.

Good news, sports fans! Just as a shrewd trade can boost the pitching staff of your favorite baseball team and positively impact the old win/lose record, good hires can help improve your own game stats as well. Here is where hiring to fit can be either a brilliant move or a terrible idea.

If you have a great team and are careful not to contaminate it through careless hiring, then hiring to fit makes sense. Beware, though, that every crew has a "collective personality" that flavors the atmosphere and is immediately perceived by the customer. It is also perceived by the rest of the team. Make enough poor hiring decisions and not only will you lose customers, your winners also will begin to feel out of place and move on to somewhere they fit again.

On the other hand, if you are unhappy with your present crew, you can raise the level of the water by hiring not to fit the personality of the team, but rather to fit the profile of the ideal. If you find yourself in this position because you inherited a crew of Bart Simpsons, hang on. You can make a difference.

If you are responsible for hiring a team of underachievers, then there is bad news for you. You are the problem. And the worse news is that people tend to hire in their own image. That rude person over there on the telephone could be you without the suit. Keep it up, pal, and they'll come and take your suit!

WHAT WERE THEY THINKING?

One of our guests was on the phone battling with a car rental company. Our guest was getting rather hot under the collar and said, "Don't you know you're in the service business?" The car company representative replied, "No, I'm in the rental car business." (Lisa Smith, Country Garden Inn, Napa, CA)

13

MARKET IT LIKE THERE'S NO TOMORROW!

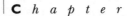icroBranders employ four sim-
ple but brain-and-foot-intensive techniques to build their brands:

1. Strategic networking
2. Clever PR
3. Event marketing
4. Positively Outrageous Service

STRATEGIC NETWORKING

My biggest weak spot as a MicroBrander is my total distaste for networking. You may feel the same, but as I've said elsewhere in this book,
if it was easy everybody would be doing it. The four requirements of
strategic networking are:

1. Be there.
2. Target your mark.
3. Be of value.
4. Follow up relentlessly.

Be There

Be where? That's the question. Be where your customers are. Eat where they eat. Support causes they support. Meet them where they work and play.

Where many of us make our mistake is in assuming that we can't be everywhere and therefore we miss too many opportunities. Epidemiologists have discovered what can be called the small world phenomenon. Essentially, what they discovered is that a virus spreads much faster in societies that are loosely organized than in societies where folks follow a more structured routine.

If you think of branding as spreading an idea virus, then the small world phenomenon applies. Rather than participating in the same organizations and sitting at the same table with the same crowd month after month, spread yourself around. Attend one group this month; pick another for your attention the next. And never, ever sit with the same folks more than two meetings in a row.

Target Your Mark

The pros of strategic networking know who they would like to meet long before the magic date arrives. Strategic networkers actually attend with a well-developed strategy. It makes them more efficient! While you are sitting with the retired couple you met last month, the strategic networker is fishing where there are actually fish!

For any business there exists a group of individuals who can do more than the average person to positively influence the enterprise. Who are your influentials? Right now, make a list of the two- or three-dozen persons who could most positively influence your cause. Make a point of communicating in at least some small way on a regular basis, so that you can remain top of mind.

Be of Value

This is the hard part that separates the amateur from the pro. The pro does more than ask to be connected. The pro becomes the connector working to bring value to the targeted mark. Before you can effectively network, you must discover how you can bring value to those you meet. Give them a reason to remember you.

Follow Up Relentlessly

If you were to approach me at a speaking engagement and ask for a business card, I would pat my pockets, look slightly embarrassed, and tell you I am certain I do not have a card on me at the moment. I could tell you that even without the show of pocket patting, because I do not have business cards.

I do not want to give you a card so you can call me to inquire about booking me. I want your card! I'll do the follow-up. If I gave you a card, there is an even chance that you will get home, discover my card in your pocket, and wonder why it's there. But when I get home, I'll know exactly why I have your card (it will be written on the back) and I will follow up.

If you are in sales, and that is all of us, and you do not have a computerized contact database management program such as ACT! or Goldmine, you are not serious about building your brand. If you are really serious, you will have and use a headset, so that while we are talking on the phone you can be keying important information about our relationship. You don't need a photographic memory so long as you have a computer, a headset, and a keyboard!

Our rule is that every contact in our database must have the next touch point scheduled. It may be a phone call, an e-mail, or even a personal visit—if you are in my database you are going to hear from me.

CLEVER PR

There is only one point to public relations: Positive publicity that is free. It's as simple as that. And that's the good news. The bad news is that getting great PR is difficult. It requires effort, imagination, timing, persistence, technique, and effort. (I know I wrote effort twice, but I want you to get the idea that the PR machine isn't something that runs on batteries. It's tough.)

The secret to getting response to your PR is timeliness. Reporters don't create the news, they follow it. So whatever news takes control of the media, tie your efforts into the news. Oh, yes, did I mention that above all, PR must be honest? Give them a great story but don't stretch the truth—just gently hype it.

Let's look at a few top stories to see how this works.

For a car dealership: *"Local Man Scores Points with NBA!"* Follow this with a story about how a car dealership is offering a $1,000 donation in the name of car buyers who can match the free throw percentage of the favorite NBA team.

For a plumbing service: *"Plumber Flushed in Water Fight."* The story reports how a local plumber has gone to bat for water rights in the area by running for a seat on the water commission.

Get the idea? Use your imagination and tie to what is in the news. All you have to do is get close.

A giant obstacle to innovation is not a lack of ideas, it is fear. People don't do or even think of things worthy of media notice for one reason—they think people will laugh at them. Great!

I Want to Be a Loser!

If there has ever been a better example of POS guerrilla-style marketing, I haven't seen it. KFC gets the prize!

Just in from the *Promo Xtra* e-zine is an announcement that KFC is piggybacking on Donald Trump's reality show, *The Apprentice,* by extending a job offer to the runner-up.

For one week and a spicy $25,000 salary, the runner-up will be offered a stint for a week in the office of the company's chief sales officer where he or she will help introduce KFC's new Oven Roasted chicken line. And did we mention the bonus? A year's supply of KFC products.

Come Mir!

It takes a lot of chutzpah to dream up really great publicity hooks. Imagine walking in to your boss and saying, "Boss, I've got a great idea for generating tons of free, positive publicity. Let's float a giant target in the ocean near New Zealand with our logo on it. Then, if a falling space station drops out of the sky and hits the target, we'll give everyone a free taco. What do you think?"

Would you have tried it? That's exactly what some genius at Taco Bell did when the Soviet Space Station Mir was about to de-orbit and crash to the earth. I saw at least three prime-time mentions of the offer on NBC, and I imagine there were countless others.

The Mir stunt was exactly the kind of thinking I would expect from a MicroBrander, yet here it was coming from a global competitor. Taco Bell was part of Tri-Con at the time, whose other two players were Pizza Hut and KFC. Imagine that! A big player dabbling in what my friends Mark and Jeff Slutsky call *Streetfighter Marketing* (Lexington Books, 1995).

Betting on a falling space station is exactly the kind of thinking you'd expect from an entrepreneur with empty pockets but not from a big-budget player like the Bell. Maybe this should be a warning; it looks like the big guys are learning to think small.

When I researched this project I went to the source, Taco Bell. And I learned that for the cost of a full-page color ad in the *Los Angeles Times,* which was in the neighborhood of $60K–$80K, Taco Bell got an estimated 120 million impressions! The readership of the Southern California edition of the *Sunday LA Times* is just over four million. In the simplest terms, Taco Bell enjoyed a leverage on its efforts that was at least 30 times greater than traditional advertising. At least. But we think it was a lot more.

Would you notice a one-time full-page ad in your local paper? Maybe, maybe not. But if you saw the president of Taco Bell on the *Today Show,* complete with footage of a target floating in the Pacific, my dollar says you would notice and probably even talk about it!

Reporters, like the rest of us, will take the easy way out, every time. If the story you want them to promote for you is going to take a lot of work on their part, the only answer you could reasonably expect is: Next! In newsrooms large and small, there's one piece of equipment that sits next to the fax machine, the trash can. Most press releases never make it beyond the trash can.

And e-mail is not even that glamorous. Like the rest of us, reporters and editors read their e-mail with one finger on the delete key. Fail to impress in the first three seconds and another electron stream bites the dust.

You have to make it easy. You have to answer the question of what's in it for you and what's in it for the audience.

Commercials and Coupons

It seems that 99.9 percent of marketing people can't think beyond those two budget-busting, tired ideas. Worse, it seems that instead of thinking of really creative ways to attract attention, the trend is to go for large production budgets and deeper discounts. Remember, anyone can give away product; it takes brains to sell it.

Recently, a major corporation announced to its operating staff that due to marketing intelligence (an oxymoron) "we have discovered that our major competitor will soon announce an ad campaign that features deep discounts. To preempt this action, we are revising our marketing plan to include an all-new promotion with even deeper discounts."

OK, let's see a show of hands. How many of you pay retail for pizza? Amazing! There are only two hands up. You, sir, may go to the restroom without permission. And you, the guy with the fake nose and glasses . . . oh, you were just kidding? Thank you!

Discount and it won't be long before the customer figures out what your product is really worth!

If you must discount, do this:

Give something free with the full-price purchase of some regularly offered item. Do not interpret this to include "buy one, get one" or other similarly stupid ideas.

Give a discount for purchases of a package of compatible items. For example, a complete start-up personal computer system might be priced lower than the individual items.

Do not:

- Offer a discount for reduced service, buying during off-hours, and so on. Customers will quickly focus on the discounted price as the "true value" of your product.
- Offer a discount on a temporarily stocked item that is not of your usual high quality. Build a reputation for quality and stick to it. Why train customers to believe that less than optimum quality is acceptable to you or to them?
- Offer discounts or hold sales on a predictable basis. Do this and you risk training your customers to wait for the sale.

Now that you have a catalog of what not to do, where do you go for ideas that work? Easy! Open your eyes and ears and creative ideas will find you. Look to your customers, employees, vendors, your industry association, and other businesses (related or not). Customers are a dynamite source of creative ideas. Find out what turns on your customers and design a promotion that ties in your business with their interests.

We discovered that many of the customers at our first restaurant were involved in providing emergency services and created a Firemen's

Olympics promo that brought a dozen fire trucks to our property and drew hundreds of curious onlookers.

Given ownership to create promotional ideas, employees will overcome their reluctance to propose anything that's truly outrageous and surprise you with an increased sense of creativity in other areas of the job. When they get more playful with your everyday customers, they enhance your company's image as a fun, friendly place to do business.

Your vendors also are a source of promotional ideas that work. After all, they service many other companies that are in the same or similar business as you. Truly heads-up suppliers make it their business to be concerned about your success. And they will be thrilled that you asked for assistance.

When we were doing our product tasting at Ben E. Keith Company, who will be one of our food vendors for the new restaurant, Dave Walsh suggested that the bartender be the person to add the final touch of whipped cream to our desserts. He went on to explain that when the waiting customers see the delectable delights, they remember to leave room for dessert. Brilliant!

If you are not a member of your industry association—no, make that *active participant* in your industry association—then shame on you! Certainly, many associations are not truly serving the needs of their members, but that is not cause for abandonment. Get in there, pay your dues, and earn the right to do more than raise a little hell. Shake 'em up!

Even if you are the industry leader, participate and participate big. You want all of your competition to at least be "pretty good," and the association is there to try to raise the standards. Besides, all the truly great ideas don't come from the big guy. Associations create the benefit of being able to share ideas with your peers and to learn from experts brought in from the outside. Your association should be a veritable fountain of ideas for promotions.

Sometimes when you have a particular problem or a specific need for a promotion, the best thing to do is to look at some totally unrelated industry and ask how would they do it. You might be surprised at how, with very little adjustment, you can create an exciting promotion.

We've received several letters over the years from folks who have adapted our ideas—and made them better! Have fun! Get those creative juices working!

14

POS MARKETING

When we discovered the value of surprising our guests by delivering just a little more than they expected, we began to look for more ways to make them say, "WOW!" Then we surprised ourselves at the many ways it could be done.

Surprises are not only fun, there seems to be no end to the creative ways you can pull them off. One of the best ways to attract attention and build sales is through fun. And there are four simple tactics for improving your relationship with your customers through marketing:

1. Have fun.
2. Get people to your property.
3. Involve the product.
4. Do something good for others.

JUST FOR THE FUN OF IT!

Fun is a serious business tactic? You bet! In fact, fun is the number-one way to get the customer involved with the product and the servers.

If you are tired of Southwest Airline stories, don't blame me! Get out and have some fun with your customers, and I'll write about you! In the meantime, check out these fun ideas.

To inaugurate four new flights between Los Angeles and Las Vegas, Southwest hosted a dozen or so Elvis wannabes to a trip to the Golden Nugget casino. At the gate, the Elvi (that's plural for you know who) treated a huge crowd of the curious to crooning and posturing. The youngest Elvis was barely seven years old, and an elderly version of the departed hero rounded out the pack. On the flight, customers were treated to preflight announcements performed to the tune of "All Shook Up" plus a few spontaneous renditions by the "real" impersonators.

Now that's not what you would expect on a typical airline. But then, there is nothing typical about Southwest, not even the planes. Southwest has a plane painted to look like Shamu the killer whale and another decked out like the flag of Texas.

Remember, the best way to know if your marketing is Positively Outrageous is to ask yourself this question: "Is it newsworthy?" As surely as you want your customers to have stories to tell, if a reporter were presented with your idea, the first question out of the box would be whether or not the story was "man bites dog" or just another ho-hum, "dog bites man."

The media are a cinch to attract and work with, as long as you keep their needs in mind. They want an interesting story, and they want to get it as easily as possible. If you have an interesting story, the media folks appreciate your call or news release. If you don't have a truly newsworthy piece, don't call the media. First of all, that's not the way to cultivate trust and friendship, and second, if you become a pest you may find yourself getting coverage you don't want.

You can help out by providing a clear and complete fact sheet for your event. If you can write an interesting news release, do it. Media people are just like the rest of us. They are overworked and underappreciated. If you want to write the entire story and hand it to them labeled as a press release, do it. You may be surprised to see it printed word for word. And best of all, they will be your words.

When you are interviewed, be certain to answer the questions that the public needs answered or that you want to answer. Just because a reporter fails to ask the right questions doesn't mean that you shouldn't go ahead and answer them anyway! Remember, reporters may be covering a dozen other stories and may not always share your enthusiasm for telling your story.

Any use of the media is a form of marketing. Any form of marketing contributes to your brand. So be careful that even your commercial advertising reflects your corporate values and corporate personality.

Here are a few of our commercials from our first restaurant:

Fishin' Fun

Hi! This is Scott from Church's Chicken. Ah . . . I know you haven't heard from me in a while. I, ah, went to Europe. Yeah, that's right . . . uh, to have lunch with . . . Princess Diana. I came back on the *Queen Mary* . . . nice boat. And she's a nice girl, too. Now while I was on the *Queen Mary,* I was fishing—from the stern—and I caught the most wonderful fish. And I brought some back for you! You know, I don't really *like* fish, but *this* is good stuff. We only serve the very best up at Church's. It's light and flaky and white and moist on the inside and kind of crisp on the outside with a wonderful, wonderful lemon seasoning. It's really, really good stuff. I mean you're gonna love it . . . even if you don't like fish, you're gonna love it. And if you do like fish . . . Whoa! This stuff is gonna send you to the moon.

All right, so I was kind of fibbing about the *Queen Mary* and all. I actually went over on the . . . Concorde. Yeah, that's right. They let me pilot it, and we caught the fish with nets. They were flying fish.

This is Scott at Church's Chicken. Don't forget to love one another!

More Fish

Hi! This is Scott at Church's Chicken. See? I told you our new fish was some kind of wonderful. And now you've tried it and realize that maybe fish isn't so bad after all. So, just to make things interesting, I have another deal for you.

Order any of our terrific fish specials and you can add an ear of corn for the great big bank-busting price of a quarter. Now I know that corn is a vegetable, but it isn't like I was trying to feed you broccoli or some other green stuff that tastes like weeds.

No, this is corn on the cob. Big, juicy, sweet, and delicious. You liked the fish, so trust me on the corn. Heck, I think corn is really some kind of fruit that some high school science teacher misclassified as a vegetable. Plus, the corn you get at Church's isn't that little weenie stuff they sell at other places.

Now you just ride on over to Church's and have yourself some more of that delicious fish and add in a big juicy ear of corn for a quarter. For a measly quarter, you can throw it out if it doesn't suit you, and at least you'll be able to look your mama straight in the eye when she asks if you've been eating your vegetables.

See you at Church's . . . and don't forget to love one another!

The commercials that ring the bell today are those that tell stories and invite the customer to participate at least vicariously. Commercials that talk about price, product, packaging, and place will always be a part of the media landscape, but commercials that tell a story or make us laugh are more in keeping with these times when customers will only trade their attention for an experience.

Add fun to your daily routine and watch productivity soar. I know, on the face of it, when people are having fun they're not working. Not true. When people are not having fun, they are thinking about anything but work. Fun and a little competition make the day go faster as well as put a little spring in everyone's step.

So here's an example of how to sponsor events that get people to your property. Too often, we are tempted to sponsor events that take place somewhere else. Bad idea!

When the March of Dimes asked us to help sponsor their annual walk by providing T-shirts, we said a quick and final, "No!" "Gee, we didn't expect that you would say no. You say yes to almost anything in the community."

That may be true, but we only say yes to things that help both the community *and* our business. So we said, "We'll be happy to sponsor the March of Dimes, just not with T-shirts. Why don't you let us help you lay out the route? It can start here, and we'll give everyone a hot honey-butter biscuit to start. It can end here, too, and we'll give everyone who finishes a refreshingly cold glass of iced tea. And we'll even have the Chicken Man lead the march." At that last statement, she said, "You could do that?" "Sure can!"

I looked really cool in the Chicken Man suit. I wore yellow knee socks, orange shorts, custom fur wings, a rubber beak, wraparound mirrored sunglasses, and to top it off, a hard hat on which we had stuffed and mounted a real chicken! It was a cool suit. (When we sold the restaurant, Buns made me keep the suit. She likes me to wear it around the house sometimes!)

Our attitude is that if we can get our product into your mouth, you will be our customer. So the goal of any promotion is to get you to our property to sample our product. Notice, please, how well our offer served both our needs and the needs of others. A promotion that doesn't benefit your business may cause you *not* to be around next year when they need you again!

INVOLVE THE PRODUCT

So maybe your property doesn't lend itself to a customer visit. Before you dismiss the idea, consider having an event at your place of business. And make sure that your place represents you well. But here is an absolute: Never do a promotion that does not involve your product.

At our business, we didn't do any promotion that didn't in some way involve our product. We had customers eat our product, wear it, swim in it, push it, and spit it, but always the product was involved.

My favorite promotion had to be our crowing for biscuits promo. Our franchisor decided to offer a nine-piece combo with two sides for $9.99. It did not include biscuits, so we decided to throw in the biscuits for another dollar or make them free to anyone who was willing to crow.

Now this was not a particularly pretty promotion. It turned out that the folks in Kerrville were predisposed to crowing. Judging by the response we got, folks must have had one heck of a pent-up desire to crow. We would say, "Would you like to add the biscuits? They're four for a dollar or free if you crow."

"You mean crow like a rooster?"

"Yes, ma'am, unless you have special training in crowing like a rabbit, a rooster version will be just fine."

Well, they would get their little feet scratching, flapping their wings and bobbing their heads like they had been preparing for years. Then they would rear back and let loose with a sometimes bloodcurdling crow, followed by a slightly embarrassed look that begged for an ovation.

One lady crowed in her car while sitting at the drive-thru. First she looked in her back seat (to see if she was alone), and then she let loose a crow that rattled windows for blocks. When she calmed down, she asked, "OK, where are my biscuits?" I said, "Ma'am, I believe you must have laid them on the seat of your car!"

For months after the promo ended, we still had customers who would come in to crow for us!

Another way to involve your product is to leverage your expertise by donating your time and talent, which have residual value to both the public you serve and your company. As an added benefit, donating yourself is a much more tangible expression of your concern for the community than the donation of dollars. Dollars are soon melted into the general fund account and their source becomes obscured, a fact that does not serve your need nearly as well as leveraging product and service.

DO SOMETHING GOOD FOR OTHERS

The best marketing tactic is doing something good for others. Call it the Law of Harvest or heads-up marketing. Doing something good for others comes right back at you. If you are the nicest person on the planet, you'll want your marketing to do something good for others. If you are the scum of the universe, you'll want to market the same way simply because it's darned good business.

Muriel Siebert & Company made "charity marketing" a way of business and a way of life. Siebert sold new issues of securities in underwriting, which by itself is nothing out of the ordinary. What is special is her promise to donate part of her profits on each sale to a charity of choice.

Typically, Siebert donated one half of the commissions received, less clearing costs. To date, Siebert and her clients have sent generous checks to such causes as Habitat for Humanity, Citymeals-on-Wheels, Los Angeles Philharmonic, and the University of Pittsburgh.

Other companies have found that charity marketing is as good for the soul and the team as it is for the bottom line.

Southwest Airlines has made its affiliation with the Ronald McDonald House a priority. There was a memorable commercial with Herb Kelleher saying, "We came over to fix dinner for friends and ended up falling in love."

You'll fall in love, too, when you put the corporate heart and pocketbook to work for good causes.

Have fun, get people to your property, involve the product, and do something good for others. That's the recipe for marketing that gets attention and builds relationships.

I walked into our restaurant and immediately noticed a woman reading our Pride Wall, a small bulletin board where we post newspaper clippings and other evidence of community involvement.

"Excuse me. I'm the owner of this chicken outfit and it makes me nervous to see my customers waiting."

"Oh, I know you," she interrupted. "You're Scott Gross. I'm waiting for my okra to cook. They told me you don't like to have it up in the afternoon, because it gets cold. They promised me it would be worth the wait, so I don't mind waiting at all."

"Well, they told you the truth but I still apologize for the wait."

"I don't mind, and I want to tell you how happy I am that you have great fried chicken."

"I'm glad we have good product, too. Why are you so happy?"

"I'm happy because of all the good things you do in this community. I'd have to eat here even if it wasn't."

Over the eight years we owned our restaurant, we did a variety of events, some bizarre ideas, but all were fun and helped build our reputation for being a great place to work and a great partner in the community.

GET SOMEONE ELSE TO PAY FOR YOUR PROMO

Yes, that's right! If you'll just look around, you'll find true partners who will share the profits and the risks. If you have an event that is going to draw hundreds, perhaps thousands, of people to your location, neighboring businesses will also benefit. Ask and chances are they will help pay. One of our best events was the Great Ping-Pong Promo.

We decided to drop 3,000 Ping-Pong balls on our parking lot, each good for a prize. We went to neighboring businesses and literally sold ad space on Ping-Pong balls. Each ball was numbered. Customers who retrieved a ball had to take it to the center court of the mall, where they could check their numbers to see which merchant they were to visit for their prize. At the merchant's, they were given a card good for a free drink at our restaurant, in addition to the merchant-supplied prize. That created incredible traffic for us and marked the beginning of a series of similarly bizarre promotions, as well as a string of incredible sales increases. Our share of the expense was less than $250!

The promotion also netted us media attention! We were on the front page of the local newspaper and even made the ten o'clock news in San Antonio with our video segment. You can't beat fun! It wins every time!

REWARD EVERYONE IF POSSIBLE

Promotions that offer only a few opportunities to win often end up disappointing many who perceive themselves as losers. The best promotions are those in which everyone is a winner.

We were approached by the school district to provide rewards for students who qualified for the honor roll. That's an admirable thing to do, but what about the thousands of kids who are trying and for one reason or another haven't managed to make the grade?

We decided to create a Pays for As program in which each student would receive a business card-sized coupon good for one to ten free drinks. The teachers circled one free drink for each A on the report card.

True, some bright youngsters came in and proudly ordered a half-dozen or more free drinks for themselves and friends or family. (It was also good to see the smile on the face of the kid who only qualified for a single drink. That may have been his first A ever. Hopefully, because it was possible for everyone to come out a winner, it wouldn't be his last.)

DON'T ALWAYS TRY TO MAKE MONEY

Occasionally, you need to run a promotion "just because." Maybe it's to say thanks to your customers. Maybe it's just to say thanks. Our favorite "just because" promotion was called the Wing and a Prayer Celebration. In-house we called it our Belly and Soul Promo. In a few words, on Christmas Day, with the help of volunteer employees, family, and customers, we cooked hundreds of dinners and gave them to local church groups to be delivered as they saw fit.

We told them, "We'll fill the belly if you will fill the soul. Find hungry people and define hunger any way that works for you." We wanted our recipients to not only be fed physically but spiritually as well. A personal visit on Christmas Day to a lonely recipient would warm several hearts, we believed.

Here's a letter to the editor from the pastor of one of the participating churches:

> Restaurant owners and staff deserve thanks. I would not want another Christmas season to go by without expressing our special thanks to the owners, Scott and Melanie Gross of our city, for their annual exhibit of Christian charity and concern for the hungry of our community.
>
> How fortunate we are to have people like these as part of our community. Thank you!

Try to pay for that kind of publicity. You can't. Besides, there's plenty of value in doing something nice just because.

For you hard-nosed businesspeople, it should be said that for that kind of promotion we still get thanks. Our customers thanked us at the cash registers, and occasionally they'd let us know their patronage was due to more than good products and friendly service.

HAVE SPECIFIC AND MEASURABLE GOALS

We spent thousands on display advertising and radio before we discovered that it had been an absolute and total waste of money.

Our worst failure was a display ad featuring a coupon redeemable for a free order of french fries with any purchase. I calculated that we spent $141.50 for each order of free french fries. What a colossal waste!

Since the french fry fiasco, I have often wondered what kind of response we would have had if we had taken the same budget, converted it into crisp $5 bills, and simply dropped them into carryout bags at random. We could have attached a card that read, "Thanks for being our customer. Please use this to treat a friend on your next visit." I'll bet the word of mouth would have been phenomenal. (Maybe we'll try that at Sporty's.)

Several times a year we used coupons. When we did, we measured them carefully. We had a hit list of our top ten coupon offers and would always lead with three and experiment with the fourth position on the sheet, in hopes of finding another winner.

As with any promotion, we forecast sales without coupons, compared that with sales with coupons, factored in distribution and the discount costs to determine the true value of the promotion. Note that the only reason we were concerned with the number of coupons redeemed was to determine which coupons worked best. What mattered was the increase in sales. We knew to use coupons to remind customers who hadn't been in for a while to come and see us again. We only needed to remind them of our quality products and friendly service.

GRABBERS

Everything that happens, everything that contributes to the customers' experience of your service or product is marketing. Everything.

Smart marketers manipulate the environment to create minievents or experiences with the idea in mind that customers will tell stories about their visit. We call these minievents "grabbers."

Grabbers are unusual, often out-of-context experiences. They may be purely visual or they can involve the server. They can be as simple as choosing an unusual name for a product. We had trouble moving dark pieces of chicken, so we ran a special on "three-legged" chickens. It helps if you make up a little story to give the customer a verbal framework for the story you want *them* to tell.

"How's a three-legged chicken taste?"

"Well, we don't really know. They're so fast that this is the first time we've been able to catch one!"

(Remember Michael Hurst's addition of "bugs" to his menu? It worked well for him, too!)

As long as we're out to lunch, here are a few out-to-lunch restaurant names that single-handedly lasso customers:

- Aunt Chovy's Pizza, Mar Vista, CA
- Thai Me Up Café, Los Angeles, CA
- Bermuda Schwartz, Winnipeg, Canada
- Mei Luck, San Antonio, TX

Grabbers can come in any form. The Piggly Wiggly Supermarket in St. Charles, Louisiana, borrowed football jerseys from the local high school team and wore them the day before the opening game to show their support and team spirit.

If you show up at the Western Heritage Credit Union in Alliance, Nebraska, on your birthday, the computer will alert the employees and you will find yourself serenaded by an impromptu all-kazoo band. Now that will get you talking!

Yogi!

His name is Yogi. And if you ask him, he is the best cabbie in all of Chicago. I haven't had the opportunity to ride in Yogi's cab, but if my mail is any indication, he must be one heck of a marketer. Several folks have sent me copies of a newspaper article describing a ride with this fantastic freeway flyer.

Yogi decorates his cab to suit the season. At Christmas he wears a Santa hat and manages to string lights throughout the interior of what would otherwise be nothing more than another cab. Once he has you inside, Yogi takes it on himself to see to your entertainment. He makes full use of the tape deck, acting as a driving DJ and taking care that you hear at least one commercial message that reminds you that you have been fortunate to have been selected for the "best cab ride in Chicago." Yogi does his level best to keep the promise. What a showman!

Bon Jour!

"Bon jour! This is Pierre, the chef. I've just finished the last two days baking. You must try my fresh French baguettes. They're waiting for you either through room service or at Chez Colette. Bon appetit!"

So goes the French-accented recording that serves as a wake-up greeting for guests at the Hotel Sofitel in Minneapolis. (Any ideas what it does for the sale of pastries?)

American Greeting

Flight 227, January 18, 1993, San Antonio to DFW

"Hey, it's me again. The temperature at this altitude is right at 61 degrees below zero. So we ask that you keep your hands and arms inside.

"At takeoff we weighed just over 300,000 pounds. Forty-eight thousand pounds was fuel, 4,000 was baggage and, between you and me, we weighed in at about 22,000 pounds, which probably indicates it's time for me to go on a diet!

"We took off at 173 miles per hour and are doing about 521 miles per hour at the moment. That's not any record, but it sure beats the old Volkswagen!"

Delta Was Ready before I Was!

The good folks at Delta Airlines helped to sponsor a seminar put on by my friends at the Orlando/Orange County Convention and Visitors Bureau. Part of Delta's contribution was to provide my air travel. After I presented Positively Outrageous Service to nearly 800 enthusiastic folks, Delta decided to try out the concept—on me!

As the seminar was about to end, I was told that Delta had called to say that my flight had been changed. They had found room for me on a flight that left later but arrived in New York, my next stop, earlier than the previously scheduled flight. Nice surprise! But the real surprise came when handing in my old boarding passes for reissue. The new ones put me in first class! They love to fly . . . and it shows!

An Army of Marketers

These ideas were sent by Ron Litchfield of Burlington, Iowa, on how Hardees makes Positively Outrageous Marketing work in its community. Ron picked his top ten and sent them along. We chose the most memorable:

1. On National Guard Day, the Iowa National Guard held its monthly training event in Hardees parking lot! It started at 6 AM one foggy March morning and used M16s to secure the lot, with big equipment at the edge of the lot for display. Drivers stopped to gawk, while the radio station did a live report that brought even more watchers.

   The marketing benefit was a newspaper story featuring a picture with Hardees' cup and more interest in joining the Guard that day than in previous several months.

   Cost: Lunch for 30 plus five rolls of film, which brought people in again the following Saturday when the pictures were posted.
2. Hardees held a Saturday Seventies live remote starting at 6 PM through midnight, complete with shag carpet, Lava lamps, pet rocks, and a disco ball from the pole sign. Employees dressed for the event. There were even contests for the first customer with a mood ring and other era mementos. The competition thought they looked silly, but sales were killer.
3. On Valentine's Day, Hardees sold heart-shaped cookies with proceeds to Warm a Heart, a power bill assistance program.
4. When the circus came to town, Hardees held a circus party and invited the circus to bring a couple of acts—and packed the store.
5. Hardees has hosted area high school homecoming kickoff parties and pony rides, washed windows at the drive-through, and even did a live remote with the radio DJ making biscuits.

Moo Mondays

This story was sent in by Vern Lindsey of Knoxville, Tennessee. "At my small gourmet ice cream store in Knoxville, Tennessee, called Hilton Head Ice Cream, I am always looking for ways to be different from the competition. When I heard your story about making people 'cluck' for their free biscuit, I thought that was great. It was a fun idea and the customer got something free that gave them something to talk about. I started thinking about how I could put something like that into motion at the ice cream store and came up with 'Moo Monday.'

"I had a large professional sign made to hang behind the ice cream cabinets. It showed the head of a cow with a cartoon-style voice circle (to show the cow was talking) and it read:

MOO MONDAY

Moo like a cow on Monday and get your ice cream at Half-Price!
"The caption underneath read: *(Must Be Convincing)*

"We are doing a little more business than on previous Mondays, even after giving 50 percent off. We expect as we get into summer this year it will create quite a buzz."

P *OS* **P** *o i n t*

What marketing events can you create to put you top of mind with your customers that will be fun and profitable?

THE MANAGER'S TOOLBOX

15

THE MANAGER'S TOOLBOX

Every human resources professional worthy of a paycheck eventually faces up to the task of predicting human behavior. And why not? The dollars, effort, and even heartache invested in hiring and attempting to train new employees who wash out of the program amounts to a staggering drain on corporate resources. The cost to companies that practice body-snatch hiring techniques and sink-or-swim training must be even greater, although infinitely more difficult to calculate.

When it was my turn in the box, I turned to Joy Wright, president of PSI in Richland Hills, Texas. Joy is a master at predicting the success rate of new hires. If you don't know Ms. Wright, or someone like her, you should. Otherwise, you are wasting big dollars on turnover that could be spent on more effective training or—here's a novel concept—dollars that could fall to the bottom line.

Wasn't it Ogilvey, the famous marketer, who said: "Only 15 percent of my marketing works? The problem is, I don't know which 15 percent!" Have you ever hired a new employee with the expectation that he would fail? Of course not (suspicion maybe, but expectation, never)! Your problem, like Ogilvey's, is that while you know not every new hire will work out, you don't know which will and which will not.

Don't get the wrong idea. Even practiced social scientists like Ms. Wright and crew cannot predict success or failure with absolute certainty. What they can do is give you very accurate measurements of character traits that are important to success in any particular job. They can develop a profile of successful candidates against which you can compare potential new hires. The closer the match, the greater the likelihood of success.

Oh sure, there will be the odd individual who profiles well but insists on crashing and burning. And there will be the applicant given a whole forest of red flags who slips through the system, gets hired, and succeeds in spite of himself. But those exceptions are rare. The rule is that once you have identified the character traits of successful individuals, the closer the new hire matches that profile, the greater are the chances for success.

It's important to note that there is no such thing as a "generic" profile of the perfect new hire. Success is always defined in terms of the job. Would you really expect someone who matched the profile of a successful nightclub bouncer to match the profile of a successful Yoga instructor? Of course not!

If you haven't developed a profile for successful entry-level employees for your organization or at least given it some serious thought, you'd better get to it. If demographers are right, there will be a tremendous shortage of labor in the United States. Success will belong to those who are able to outhire, outtrain, and outretain the competition.

To help you with your project, I asked Ms. Wright to develop a profile of someone likely to have a high tolerance for customer contact. If you don't at least start by hiring people who crave customer contact, your chances of providing good service are slim, and the likelihood you'll ever achieve Positively Outrageous Service are absolutely nil.

POSITIVELY OUTRAGEOUS SERVICE MANAGEMENT QUIZ AND ANALYSIS

Positively Outrageous Service begins with hiring the right individuals in the first place. We said it before: the first job of management is to assemble a team of winners. But notice, please, that the bulk of this book is devoted to managing that team.

Try your luck at the Positively Outrageous Service Management Quiz and find out just how well prepared you and your company are to deliver Positively Outrageous Service.

Positively Outrageous Service Predictor

Can you provide outrageous service?

1. I am proud of my accomplishments at work.
2. I have a great deal of confidence in my abilities.
3. I am my own best friend.
4. I enjoy projects that call for rapid action.
5. I typically do well in pressure situations.
6. I enjoy jobs that permit movement and freedom.
7. I enjoy being surprised.
8. I enjoy entertaining guests.
9. I find it easy to make new friends.
10. I have a desire to be someone who is well known and successful.
11. I would enjoy being famous.
12. People think of me as an energetic person.
13. Assuming the responsibilities of a "leader" feels comfortable to me.
14. Many of my close friends have a unique or nonconventional lifestyle.

If you responded true to 10 or more of these questions, you are confident and creative, and chances are you like people—all ingredients of outrageous talent.

If you responded true to 6–9, chances are you experience enthusiasm on a more inconsistent basis. At times, you can be better than most, and at other times you will be very reserved.

Five or fewer depict a more reserved person who may stick to the tried and true and who requires a great deal of security and conformity in life. Chances are, providing Positively Outrageous Service is not your cup of tea.

Positively Outrageous Service Management Quiz

Rate your agreement with the following statements. Give each a rating between 0 and 10.

____ 1. Executives in your organization personally and regularly serve customers.

____ 2. You have a highly visible customer feedback system that gives immediate feedback to both employees and customers.

____ 3. Stories about outstanding customer service are regular features of company communications and meetings.

____ 4. Training in your company gives service training equal importance to technical or procedural training.

____ 5. Employees from entry level up are highly empowered to make service decisions.

____ 6. Though mass marketing may be an element of the marketing strategy, event selling and other person-to-person tactics are frequently employed.

____ 7. Failure is relevant. If you are not failing at least occasionally, you probably aren't growing. First mistakes are free.

____ 8. Compensation is, and should be, directly linked to contribution.

____ 9. Change is regarded as important, and the "contrarian's viewpoint" of challenging tradition is considered praiseworthy rather than dangerous.

____ 10. When you are a customer, you "play" with clerks, attendants, waitpersons, etc.

____ TOTAL

Analysis

Statement #1: When corporate executives regularly take part in serving the customer, they are doing more than simply helping to cement a relationship with the folks who pay the bills. The less obvious benefit is by personally serving customers, executives who are the "visible standard" communicate that serving others is honorable and that customer service is the focus of corporate energy.

Statement #2: Highly visible feedback systems communicate to customers not only that they can be heard but also that the company actively solicits customer input. Feedback systems, to be effective, must get data immediately into the hands of the involved employees, so that the mental connection between behavior and consequence can be made. It is equally important to respond to the customer. Such a response rewards the customer for taking time to give input and says in no uncertain terms that the company cares.

Statement #3: Ken Blanchard talks about Legendary Service. Legends are stories told over and over about brave and wonderful deeds. It is in the telling of stories that heroes are made. Telling service stories turns ordinary clerks into heroes. Building heroes encourages future service excellence.

Statement #4: Getting it right technically almost doesn't count if the customer also receives a poor perception of commitment to a continued relationship. Training that focuses solely on the technical, procedural aspects of the business is only half done.

Statement #5: It is of little value to talk service unless employees are also empowered to, and rewarded for, delivery of Positively Outrageous Service.

Statement #6: Mass marketing techniques take on added significance when they are supplemented by event marketing. Event marketing can be done on a grand scale or it may be only a one-on-one opportunity to deliver Positively Outrageous Service.

Statement #7: Positively Outrageous Service involves an element of risk. After all, POS marketing and Positively Outrageous Service are definitely outside the norm. Managers who are punished for straying beyond "that's the way it has always been done" are not likely to try new, possibly dynamite ideas.

Statement #8: Companies where innovation is not rewarded, where longevity without contribution is prized, are not likely to make any moves to make them either outstanding or simply stand out.

Statement #9: Success will require at least some internal friction. As long as those holding on to traditions of quality and service allow at least some freedom to marketing contrarians, corporate values will not be lost; rather, they will evolve and survive.

Statement #10: This may be the single most important indicator of your personal tendency to Positively Outrageous Service. The most capable practitioners of POS are constantly inviting others to play. Play is another word for involvement. It will be the company that involves the customer in every way that creates solid, thriving relationships.

Your score? If it was 80 or higher, you are probably already marketing and serving outrageously. A score of 60 or higher puts you in the category of "interested but not yet ready to buy." A score below 60 points puts your company on the endangered species list!

TEN COMMANDMENTS FOR MANAGERS

There's no claim here that the following ten commandments should be carved in stone. But they work for me, and they may just work for you.

My list of ten is posted for all to read and each of my managers has a personal copy. They are not necessarily listed in any particular order. Just like the biblical ten, break any one and I'll personally send you at least as far as manager's purgatory.

1. Be a product, service, and cleanliness fanatic. The operating word is "awareness." Notice, please, that the commandment has two parts. It's fairly obvious, or at least it should be, that product, service, and cleanliness are the three critical elements of our business. But I'm not saying "be interested" in product, service, and cleanliness; I'm suggesting that anything less than fanaticism is a halfhearted attitude. Debbie Fields, founder of Mrs. Fields' Cookies, is quoted as having said, "good enough seldom is." Think about it.

Part two of this first commandment is "awareness." Your mission is to help your employees see opportunities for improvement. One way is to regularly inspect your operation. For maximum impact, make your inspections unannounced. And here's the big one: Tie bonuses to the inspection score. My managers receive a weekly, graded inspection. Score 80 percent and you get only 80 percent of your sales bonus. Score 80 percent very often and you get outplacement counseling.

2. Do not say, "I don't know"; say, "I'll find out." "I don't know" ranks right up there with "It's not my job." As a manager, your job is to develop a team that is so good that the operation runs without you. My team swears that things actually improve when I leave. People don't "get

better," and they don't grow when they are allowed to sit on their igno-
rance. It's okay not to know; it's not okay not to find out.

3. Do not say, "I can't"; say, "I'll learn." You can't grow strong leadership by allowing weakness. Adopt the attitude that your people can do
anything. Expect them to do it and then stand by to be surprised at how
resourceful and intelligent they prove to be. "I can't" doesn't work with
me. Ask me for training and you'll get training. Tell me you "can't," and
I'll look for someone who either can or is at least willing to learn.

**4. Always try to say "yes" to customers. Say "no" when it's for their
own good.** Two short stories will illustrate: Our first restaurant was in
a small town. For some strange reason, a large majority of our guests pay
by personal check. When we opened, we didn't accept checks. After all,
we reasoned, if you don't have $4 or $5 cash for lunch, maybe you
shouldn't be eating out! We turned away a lot of business.

Finally someone put it to me like this: "If I promised to eat at your
place once a week all year long, would you be willing to give me a 10
percent discount?"

"Sure," I said.

"If you accepted checks, how many would you expect to bounce?"

"I don't know. Maybe 1 or 2 percent."

"Instead of the 10 percent discount, can I just pay by check?"

Point made. We accepted dozens of checks each week. One or two
bounced but were quickly collected with a single phone call. Annually,
we actually lost about $100 to bad checks. But just look at all those addi-
tional sales!

Story number two: A car salesman phoned in a delivery order. He
asked for a cup of ice and was refused.

"I'm sorry, sir. Our boss doesn't allow us to deliver fountain drinks,
because the ice will melt. Guess that applies to cups of ice as well."

I hit the roof! I called, apologized, and requested that when he
called for future orders, he should identify himself as "the Ice Man
from Hillstar Motors." For six cents worth of paper and ice, we had a
twice-per-week customer.

Saying "yes" to customers is saying "yes" to business. As a side benefit, our out-of-the-ordinary service brought us even more business for
the auto dealership. Twice each month, they ordered lunch for the
entire staff. We delivered tea in gallon jugs and dropped off a cooler of
ice, which the general manager returned on his way home.

Say "no" to drugs but look for creative ways to say "yes" to customers.

5. Do not ask what to do. Decide and then do it. At worst, make several recommendations, and then act. It's impossible to build a strong team if you make all the decisions for them. Let them make a free mistake now and then if it won't be too costly. Mistakes don't really build character, but confidence and competence that arise at decision making do. Besides, the way I figure it, if I have to make all the decisions, why do I need you?

6. Ask, "Is what I am doing now improving our product, sales, service, or property?" There are thousands of things to be done in a business. Most of them count, but some do not. This is especially true when it comes to promotions and community service projects. Since it's impossible to be involved in everything or to donate to every cause, we always ask one simple question: "How does this sell product?" If the answer is, "It doesn't," we pass. There are too many things that count to waste resources on those that do not.

This is also true for remodeling ideas, staffing ideas, and wild-eyed ideas for new products and services.

7. Be a list master. When asked, "What's on your list today?" always be prepared to show your list. All of my lead people are required to carry a small pocket notebook. I carry one as well. Having a list shows you are at least thinking about the business. A list is the beginning of a plan. Without a plan, the business runs you instead of the other way around.

Employees should always have a longer list than the boss. If not, it's because:

- The boss does most of the work. Stupid . . . because if I'm working, how can I be thinking?
- The boss does not trust the employees to competently handle important projects. This is a sure sign of poor hiring and training and should cause one more project to be added to the list. Replace the boss.

8. Write every idea and promise on your list. Ideas not recorded are ideas destined to be lost. Judith Briles, a successful author, says that writing a book seems to clear her mind for more new ideas. Record your ideas as they strike and be prepared to be amazed at how many more will pop into your mind.

Here's an idea to add to your list right now. Buy a miniature tape recorder and carry it with you always. Ideas that strike while you are driving, waiting in line, or otherwise occupied won't be lost (and often turn out to be your very best!).

9. Keep all agreements completely. If you intend to keep an agreement, write it down so you don't forget. If you do not intend to keep an agreement, don't make it. Recording your ideas allows them to mellow instead of evaporate. The difference between the successful and the also-rans is not so much in the quality of their ideas. Successful people implement more ideas. They have more failures, too. But in a competitive world, a "big shot is nothing more than a little shot who kept on shooting."

10. Manage (think) first; labor second. The value of a manager lies in leadership, training, and decision making. Manual labor is part of everyone's job, but a restaurant manager washing dishes has no more value than a dishwasher washing dishes.

My managers are expected to be working managers, not nicely dressed dining room fixtures. Both my wife and I take that same hands-on approach when we are in the restaurant. In fact, one of our employees commented that he had never seen owners so willing to be physically involved. That isn't necessarily a compliment.

Leaders should always position themselves where they have the greatest customer contact and impact on service. A boss who runs to the office to do something that could be easily handled by a junior employee or could be postponed may be helping. He may also be hiding. Send someone else to the office and stay with the action where your decision making, training, and leadership can have the most impact.

TOP CAUSES OF POOR EMPLOYEE MORALE

1. Undesirable work environment
2. Improper materials or equipment
3. Lack of feedback
4. Inadequate benefits
5. Insufficient pay
6. Poor management, lack of training
7. No orientation, sales, or product training
8. Inconvenient parking
9. No organized approach or vision to direct efforts

Scott's No-Fail 10 Percent Finder

"It's not unusual to get really angry at a customer. Everyone does at one time or another. Still, there's a big difference between doing something overt like getting physical with a customer and something like gently putting a rude customer in his place.

"How many times in the last six months have you felt it was necessary to get tough with a customer?"

"Tell me about the worst incident."

TEAM MANAGEMENT DIAGNOSTIC

Employees work hard but not together.

Why . . .
- There is no sense of team . . . we didn't think to work together.
- Players distrust one another.
- Job is organized so as to discourage teamwork.

Look for . . .
- Opportunities to create teams charged with completing specific projects.
- Politics and gossip that may be breeding mistrust.
- Reward systems that promote individual performance.

Do . . .
- Begin to assign interesting projects to teams of team players.
- Refuse to tolerate third-party communication. Require speakers to include the third party in the conversation.
- Examine the reward systems and make certain that there is a strong incentive for working as a team.

Employees work hard but produce poor results.

Why . . .
- Goals are not clearly stated to those involved.
- The production system doesn't support the desired outcomes.
- Employees are not working as teams.

Look for . . .
- False goals that may have been tacitly encouraged by management.
- Faults in work design that may be working against goal achievement.
- Rewards that may be promoting counterproductive individual work.

Do . . .
- Clarify goals or set new goals.
- Help team members set daily objectives.
- Provide frequent feedback on progress to goal.
- Review the job process and correct flaws of policy, procedure, and physical operation that may be counterproductive.

Employees engage in political infighting and gossip.
Why . . .
- There is always a reward or perceived reward for any behavior including antisocial behavior.

Look for . . .
- Unrecognized, probably informal, reward systems that reward backstabbing.
- Gossipers who may be working just at or even below the level of performance required of their job.

Do . . .
- Cease to listen to or otherwise participate in gossip.
- Require that a third party be present if there is to be criticism of that party.
- Create a policy that states gossip is viewed as nonteam play and make it known that politicians will be invited to play for another team.

Teams produce erratically.
Why . . .
- Erratic performance is almost always due to misunderstood goals.

Look for . . .
- Unclear goals.
- Random changes in equipment.

- Possible consistently poor performance in one product or service area that may give the appearance that overall performance is erratic.
- Erratic presence of a conflicting goal or motivator.

Do . . .
- Graph performance to help pinpoint when and where it varies.
- Look for opportunities to clarify goals.
- Provide frequent feedback on performance.

Employees are frequently absent.
Why . . .
- People don't miss things that are fun on purpose. Absenteeism is frequently higher on Fridays and Mondays as employees stretch out their weekends.

Look for . . .
- Cycles in the work routine that correlate with absenteeism.
- Rewards or disincentives that may correlate with absenteeism.
- Opportunities to make work more like the weekend—fun.

Do . . .
- Eliminate disincentives.
- Create incentives; that is, randomly reward in some fashion folks who are present during periods associated with high absenteeism.
- Review the job design and build in opportunities for creativity and judgment; eliminate boring routine.

Excellent product; sales are down.
Why . . .
- Just because you think things are fine doesn't mandate that the customer agrees.

Look for . . .
- Unexpected new products or prices from your competition that make your product or service seem less attractive to your customer.
- Possible defects, real or imagined, that make your product less desirable.

Do . . .
- Ask verbally or via survey why and how purchasing patterns have changed.
- Look for correlations between production changes and sales.
- Look for correlations between sales and changes in the marketplace or to your customer base.

Lack of customer loyalty.
Why . . .
- Customer loyalty is not a given; it must be earned.

Look for . . .
- Reasons why your customer should be loyal to you or others.
- Ways to develop a relationship between you and your customer.

Do . . .
- Create a frequent customer program.
- Initiate regular communications to your customer even when they are not buying.
- Look for opportunities to deliver POS—and get started!

Advertising does not produce results.
Why . . .
- Four things have to happen for advertising to work. It must be desirable, exclusive, believable, and convenient. If all four of those conditions are not met in the right combinations for your market, no amount of advertising will work.

Look for . . .
- Other advertising that has captured your customers' attention.
- Details about your offer that do not match the target.
- Insufficient reach and frequency; not enough people to hear the message with a frequency great enough to matter.

Do . . .
- Ask your customers where else they shop and why.
- Research to define your target.
- Refine your offer and format to match the target.
- Focus your efforts even if it means fewer campaigns and media outlets.

Low productivity in spite of hard work.
Why . . .
- Working hard does not guarantee results.

Look for . . .
- Obstacles created by poor job design such as poor process flow or unnecessary steps.
- Antiquated or inappropriate equipment or materials.
- Little agreement on what constitutes good work.

Do . . .
- Eliminate unnecessary steps.
- Provide up-to-date technology and materials.
- Clarify what the goals are.
- Provide productivity feedback.

Employees show great resistance to change.
Why . . .
- People are not resistant to change; they resist *being changed.*
- People are more afraid of the unknown future than of the known present and are uncertain what the world will look like after the change.
- Stakeholders are not convinced that making the change will be "worth it."

Look for . . .
- Rumors that sow seeds of doubt.
- Misunderstanding about the time and process for change.
- Opportunities for selling the change.

Do . . .
- Set up easy, direct-to-the-top communication channels.
- Offer evidence that failure to change has negative consequences.
- Widen decision making to include as many players as possible.
- Leave details of the change to implementation-level players.
- Offer convincing evidence that postchange conditions will be exactly as predicted and worth the effort.

Customers report that service is not friendly.
Why . . .
- If customers say that service is not friendly, it is not friendly.

Look for . . .
- Differences between customer expectations and organization standards.
- Microinsults that may be influencing customer opinion.
- Customer service and services provided by the competition.

Do . . .
- Survey to discover exact customer expectations.
- Analyze how expectations are being managed.
- Discover and eliminate microinsults.
- Train players in customer expectations and service strategies.
- Eliminate obstacles to friendly service, such as poor hiring, poor training, and short staffing.

Customers report that service is slow.
Why . . .
- Service is not a matter of speed; it is a matter of perception.

Look for . . .
- Environmental elements that may influence the perception of speed.
- Service provided by the competition and in other industries that may not be related but may be influencing the situation.
- Discover your customer's exact expectations of service speed.

Do . . .
- Eliminate waiting where possible.
- Make waiting more interesting or pleasant where possible.
- Make waiting a benefit by providing extra service, training, etc.
- If waiting is done in person, use a serpentine queue to make waiting fairer and to make the line seem to move faster.

Customers complain that orders are often filled inaccurately.
Why . . .
- Accurate order filling is often a matter of perception.

Look for . . .
- Ways the customer contributes to the accuracy of the order.
- Ways that the system could be changed to put the customer in charge.
- Ways the system encourages error, for example, through using arcane order-units.

Do . . .
- Verify the order before filling.
- Eliminate confusing descriptions of units of measure.
- Give customers feedback on order accuracy to manage expectations.

Customers will not buy unless on "a deal."

Why . . .
- Customers, like employees, are trained in their behavior.
- Customers are not stupid. They recognize value when you tell them!

Look for . . .
- Instances where customers are being trained to expect a deal.
- Opportunities to shape customer perception of value.
- Opportunities to bundle, creating a perception of a bigger deal.

Do . . .
- Eliminate predictable discounting.
- Eliminate discounting on core products.
- Create bundles that offer discounts, where the customer has to do something extra to get something extra.
- Refuse to deal on price; deal on terms and service.
- Take advantage of every opportunity or create opportunities to make value tangible.

Employees experience a high accident rate.

Why . . .
- There are no accidents, only expected results.

Look for . . .
- Equipment or processes that contribute to accidents.
- Correlations between time, place, or product and accidents.

Do . . .
- Eliminate opportunities for accidents.
- Repair or replace equipment.
- Train players in procedures.
- Provide feedback and reinforcement for safe behavior.

Grievance rate is high.

Why . . .

- People never complain about themselves. It's always the other guy.
- When the players are in control, there is no need to complain, only a need to make things better.

Look for . . .

- Anything that fosters a "them versus us" mentality.
- Are team players in control of the work environment or is everything a matter to be decreed from on high?

Do . . .

- Shut up and listen.
- Get out with the troops and demonstrate that you understand.
- Ask for help in identifying "stupid." There will be plenty to find.
- Create ways for operatives to contribute. Ask for, then act on suggestions for improvement. Reward great suggestions.

Turnover is high.

Why . . .

- Working for you is a bore.
- Who wants to work where it's not fun?
- Stress occurs at all levels. It's the number-one cause of turnover.

Look for . . .

- Signs of repetitive, boring, and restrictive work.
- Signs that people are uncertain of what is expected of them.
- Frequent changes or inconsistent job requirements.
- Customers who are aggressive, rude, and/or overly demanding.

Do . . .

- Assign work to teams and let teams complete an entire process.
- Clarify goals.
- Provide lots of positive feedback.
- Train management to act as a team, too, to give consistent instruction.
- Review the order system to make certain that customers know how to order and that yelling is not necessary.
- Train, train, train.

Theft of time, tools, customers, and cash.
Why . . .
- People never steal from themselves. Your players have no buy-in.
- Some people are natural thieves.

Look for . . .
- Autocratic management style.
- Opportunities to rationalize theft as "getting what I deserved."
- Poor hiring practices that fail to screen thieves and drug abusers.
- Opportunities to steal without getting caught—temptation.
- An example set by management, such as golfing on company time.

Do . . .
- Move to a more democratic management style.
- Remove overt temptation temporarily.
- Set an example of scrupulous honesty in all dealings.
- Learn to screen applicants thoroughly.
- Eliminate any chance that employees are not fully paid and fairly treated.

Employees pay lip service to mission but don't act.
Why . . .
- If you don't believe it, I don't believe it.
- A fish rots from its head down, and a dead fish smells awful for a long, long time.

Look for . . .
- Example set by management.
- Disincentives for actually making the change.
- A history of inconsistency, chasing the latest management fad.

Do . . .
- Involve the team in setting the mission.
- Provide positive feedback.
- Celebrate progress and those who contribute.
- Be prepared for the change to take a long time.
- Set the example, go first, and go all the way.
- Be willing to lose a few key players.
- If you build it they will come . . . eventually.

Employees exhibit high morale, high productivity.

Why . . .
- A system left to itself will eventually run downhill.
- Leaving things well enough alone is a recipe for disaster in a changing world.

Look for . . .
- Early signs of deterioration.
- Potential for the technology or the market to mature.
- Changes in the market or technology that could make your product obsolete.

Do . . .
- Continue to celebrate successes.
- Begin to re-create yourself before being forced to do so.
- Introduce enough challenge to keep the system responsive.
- Raise the bar.

Difficulty recruiting Service Naturals.

Why . . .
- Winning team players have choices. Yours isn't the best choice.

Look for . . .
- Competing opportunities that attract your potential hire.
- Reasons why Service Naturals would not even apply with you.

Do . . .
- View recruiting as a marketing process; you need a message and a delivery system.
- Create an attractive work environment before you attempt to sell.
- Offer rewards only to the Service Naturals you have on staff for recruiting more just like them.
- Survey winning team players to find out why they were attracted to their present job.

New employees start strong but performance quickly deteriorates.

Why . . .
- You're doing a good job recruiting, hiring, and training.
- It's the management or the system that stinks.

Look for . . .
- Reasons why employees may lose their enthusiasm.

- Nonperforming old-timers who may have a reason for holding down production; for example, concern that standards will be raised.

Do . . .
- Ask your internal customers what they would change about the job.
- Create work teams responsible for entire processes.
- Provide frequent, positive feedback for performers.
- Base individual compensation in part on team performance.

Employees ignore procedures.
Why . . .
- When there are two or more competing incentives, the one that is most desirable always wins.

Look for . . .
- Ways that not following procedures are being reinforced.
- Possibility that procedures are not clearly understood.

Do . . .
- Clarify the procedures including the reasoning behind them.
- Stamp out stupid.
- Discover and eliminate the competing reinforcer for not following procedures or the punishment for doing things by the book.

Team members work hard but not together.
Why . . .
- People work together when they have both permission and purpose.

Look for . . .
- Organization quirks that may discourage teamwork.
- Potential disincentive for working together, particularly reinforcing individual performance.
- Reasons why people may not know or believe they should work together, for example, conflicting goals or personalities.

Do . . .
- Create reinforcements for teamwork.
- Promote teamwork.
- Redesign the work process to encourage teamwork.

- Consider changing players or field positions.
- Create group goals.

Workplace is cluttered with sacred cows.
Why . . .
- No one knows why sacred cows are allowed to live. They can't be shot until you find out who is the owner.

Look for . . .
- Sacred cows that have no owner. Shoot them on the spot.
- The history behind sacred cows.
- Possible benefits of allowing them to live, perhaps even fatten.
- Potential for training your sacred cows.

Do . . .
- Find the owners of sacred cows and ask if they are really sacred.
- Play "Stamp out stupid" and "Things we don't do but could."
- Think of ways sacred cows could be put to good use.
- Think of ways sacred cows could be replaced by sacred bulls.

THE 100-YEAR FIRE

When I was a kid my gran loved me more than life itself. Whatever I wanted, she wanted. In her eyes I could do no wrong, and maybe that's why I struggled to do well, so she wouldn't be disappointed.

After school I would ride my bike to Gran's house, even though I knew she would still be at work as a waitress in downtown Cincinnati. I'd let myself in (we never locked doors in those days), head for the kitchen, and then straight for the press, a small closet that more sophisticated folks might call a pantry.

Then I would choose a can of fruit cocktail or sometimes a can of peaches and sit at the small kitchen table. The sturdy wooden table was held together by many coats of white enamel paint and topped by an oil-skin cover. The quiet of the house would be broken only by the scrape of my spoon, the hum of the refrigerator, and the tick, tick, tick of the clock over the stove. It was one of those clocks shaped like a cat and had eyes and a tail that moved in opposite directions with every beat.

When I finished, I would drink the juice and leave the spoon in the can right in the middle of the table. Now, an ordinary gran might be upset that I had eaten without asking and then added insult to injury by leaving a mess. But my gran knew it wasn't a mess that I was leaving.

It was a sign. It was my way of leaving a note that said, "I was here and I was thinking of you."

Once out the door, I would fire up my trusty Schwinn and ride through the hole in the hedge that Gran let me make. She understood how tough it could be for a little guy to lift a heavy bicycle over the tall front stoop.

What goes around does indeed come around. The surprise is how quickly things come around. Yesterday, we returned home from a road trip and noticed a little blue stool had been left in front of the sink in our bathroom. This was a sure sign we had been visited by The Princess, who had washed her hands and left us a sign saying, "I was here and I was thinking of you."

In our little part of the world, tucked away in the hill country of central Texas, it doesn't often get cold. When it does, Buns makes chili and I build a fire, especially when I know Jo Bob is coming. Jo Bob loves to curl up in front of the fire. (When I call her house to announce chili and a fire in the fireplace, I always ask, "Is this my beautiful, handpicked daughterette?" Jo Bob loves to answer, "Yes!")

One of those special days while I was building the fire, the voice I love most floated in from the kitchen saying, "I see you are building a fire for your beautiful, handpicked daughterette."

"You know, Buns, this is the way my gran treated me. She was always thinking about me. Don't you know that when I am dead and gone, every time Jo Bob sees a roaring fire in a fireplace she's going to think of me?"

"She'll smile and say, 'Pops always built a fire for me whenever the weather was cold and he knew we were coming for chili.'

"Buns, this fire will burn for 100 years, because she's going to pass it on to our grandchildren and their grandchildren through a gesture of her own that makes someone else feel warm and toasty on a dreary day. A hundred years from now someone is going to snuggle close to a fire or benefit from an act of kindness and smile just because I'm hauling a little firewood tonight."

If a year or decades from now, this book, these ideas, make a difference for you, maybe you will remember that I was here and I was thinking of you.

That's POS. Pass it on.

A

Absenteeism, 194
Accidents, 199
Accomplishment, 130–31
Ackerman, Duane, 54
Acquisitiveness, 60
ACT!, 161
Advertising, 11, 195–96
  commercials, 163, 169–70
  promotions and, 173
  publicity, 162–63
Age Wave, The (Dychtwald), 61
Aging consumers, 60–63
Agreements, keeping, 191
AirFlite, 64
Albertson's, 56, 127
Albrecht, Karl, 150
American Airlines, 177
American Demographics, 60
Angel Flight, 141
Apologies, 48–50
Appreciation, 133–35
Apprentice, The, 162
Aunt Chovy's Pizza, 176
Awareness, 46, 92, 188
A&W Root Beer, 32–33
Aycock, Bill, 64

B

Ballard, Chris, 75–76
Barnum, P.T., 87
Bates, Mike, 49
Beecroft, Bruce, 19
BellSouth, 54
Ben E. Keith Company, 165
Ben & Jerry's, 20
Berghoff Brewing Company, 87
Bermuda Schwartz, 176
BIGresearch, 61
Blanchard, Ken, 98, 130, 187
Bond, Karen, 75
Borrowed Dreams (Gross), 94

Branding, 109–18
  Brand Identity Genius, 142–43
  customer perception of, 115–17
  defining and communicating
    problems, 117–18
  key ideas, 112–15
  MicroBranding, 110–18, 139, 143,
    159
  multiple brands, 115–17
  position statement, 138–40
  Showalter Flying Service, 143–46
Briles, Judith, 190
British Airways, 11–12
Brown, Ken, 22–23
Buchin, Stanly, 60–61
Buck passing, 126
Bundling, 111
Burger King, 69
Burlingame, Mary, 17
Buying power, 55

C

Calloway, Wayne, 124
Campbell's Soup, 112
Cartwright, John, 77
Category killers, 53
Cell phones, 64–65, 70
Chandler, Harry, 54
Change, 142
  resistance to, 196–97
Charitable support, 47–48, 172–73
Chocolate Soldier, 14
Choice, 95–96
Christensen, Clayton, 63
Church's Chicken, 169–70
Cialdini, Robert, 139
Clifton, Donald, 45–46
Cold Stone Creamery, 88
Comfort, 100
Commercials, 163, 169–70
Communications
  branding and, 113–14
  omnipresence of, 68

It would be hard to put the words STUFFY and T. Scott Gross on the same page. With Scott, what you see is exactly what you get—a quiet, introspective geek who somehow manages to blossom when given an hour and an audience.

Scott has been wowing clients since he first began sharing the simple secrets of Positively Outrageous Service. He has a list of clients that reads like a Who's Who of customer service. From giant internationals to small town chambers of commerce, T. Scott Gross is the name they recall when it comes to managing the customer service experience.

Scott likes to say that Positively Outrageous Service is not something you do . . . it's something you are.

Scott is rarely without his best friend on the planet, his wife and partner, Buns. You can contact them at http://www.tscottgross.com or if you are in the neighborhood of Kerrville, Texas, stop and say hey at Sporty's, A Casual Café.